BROWNIE Annual 1982

Edited by Fiona Lawson

THIS ANNUAL BELONGS TO...

£2.50

Welcome to the Magic Land of Puppets

A Visit to the Polka Children's Theatre

Words by Fiona Lawson

Photographs by David Rayfield

How would you like to spend a day in a magic land—a land full of puppets and playgrounds, toys and trains, circuses and clowns—oh yes, and a bull called Ferdinand?

Well, that's just what Sarah Evans, of the 10th Wimbledon Brownies, did one day when she went along to the Polka Children's Theatre in Wimbledon.

The Theatre really is a magical sort of place—built especially for children—and there are all sorts of surprising things going on inside!

Let's go on a trip round the theatre with Sarah, to see just what she found behind those magic doors!

1.
"Open Sesame!" Just what lies behind those painted doors? We're about to find out! You'd never guess, would you, that until three years ago this attractive theatre was an old church hall?

2.
"One for the front row, please!" Sarah's all set to enjoy the show. Up to 600 children a day visit the theatre at its busiest times. Handicapped children can join in too—the theatre has been specially equipped throughout so that they can take part in all the activities.

3.
"My name's Sarah—what's yours?" This is the theatre's famous coat rack, with pegs at different levels to suit children of all heights. He looks quite friendly, doesn't he?

4.
"We may look quiet now, but just wait till someone pulls our strings..." This is just a tiny part of the marvellous exhibition of puppets, old and new, in the main foyer. There are over 3,000 puppets to be seen – and you can actually work some of them, to make them dance and jump.

5.
"Grr! I'm Gruffy in the glass case!" Gruffy may be growly, but he's not at all scary really. He's only kept in a glass case because he's too old and valuable to touch.

6.
"Bill and Ben and a Brownie in the middle!" Sarah doesn't look very sure of Bill and Ben, but they're only cardboard cut-outs used as stage decorations. So Sarah decided to go backstage to meet some real actors...

7.
"Hello Ferdinand!" Ferdinand is the star of the show when he's acting in a play, but he's really a very shy little bull off stage. It's just as well there were a couple of human actors there to help him out!

8.
"This is much better than dressing up in mummy's old clothes at home!" In the workroom, Sarah discovers a whole pile of boxes with intriguing names like 'fur' and 'sparkly braid', and can't resist taking a peek. Well, could you?

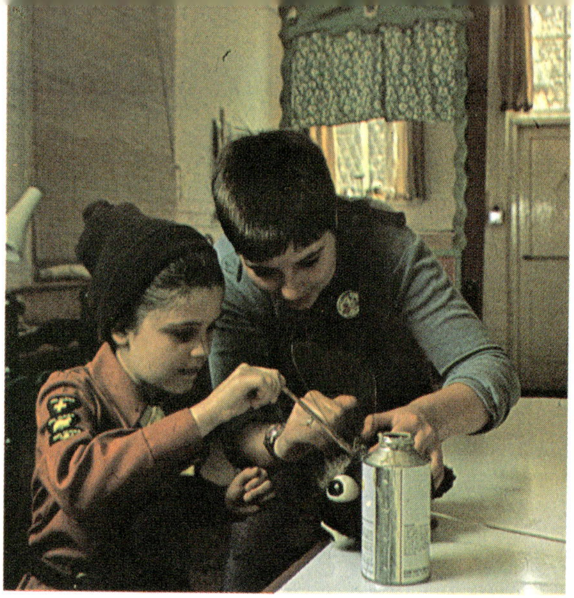

9.
"Just a dab of glue under his wing there – that's it..." Sarah gives First Aid treatment to a toy bumble bee with a broken wing. A Brownie does a good deed every day, but it's not every day you get the chance to mend a bee's wing, is it?

10.
"Say cheese." No wonder Sarah's grinning like a Cheshire cat – she has just discovered that Orlando, the playground cat, has a hollow tummy. You can reach it by climbing up the steps in his tail – and he's just the right size for a Brownie to play inside! Not only that, but his head spins round and round too!

11.
"Seesaw, jackdaw..." Can you imagine sitting on a seesaw with a giant bird at the other end? This is another attraction of the theatre's playground, which also boasts a super playhouse with a door so small that no adult could possibly get inside!

12.
"All aboard! All aboard!" Time for a rest and a snack in the café. And what a café! Delicious home-made, old-fashioned food, delivered to the front of the counter by—believe it or not—a clockwork train!

13.
"Next stop Wimbledon!" Sarah enjoys a drink in the Polka Pantry café, where the seats are in model old-fashioned railway carriages. It even has painted scenery outside the windows! And what's more, unlike a real train, it doesn't rattle about while you're eating!

14.
"Time to go home..." Sarah stops off in the theatre shop on the way home to choose a memento of her day at the fabulous puppet theatre. And guess what she picked—yes, a glove puppet! Goodbye, Polka Theatre! We'll be back soon!

The Polka Children's Theatre really is well worth a visit if you are ever near Wimbledon, but don't worry if you live too far away. The actors from the theatre have their own touring company—the Polka Company—which travels all round Britain, putting on shows in schools and local halls. Look out for them in your area.

If you would like to receive details of the Polka Club and the theatre's mailing service, send a stamped addressed envelope to: The Polka Children's Theatre, 240 The Broadway, Wimbledon, London SW19.

The Brownie Annual would like to thank all the members of the Polka Theatre's staff for their kindness and co-operation.

Look at Spring

When Spring comes, watch out for the birds nesting in the hedgerows. You may see a thrush busily building its nest, or you may spot the blue eggs of the hedge sparrow, or dunnock, on a nest in the hawthorn. Blackbirds will be nesting too, perhaps in the oak tree, and you may see the handsome magpie, in his black and white finery. Hares and rabbits feed in the meadows, and sleepy toads lie lazily in the soft sunshine. There are carpets of spring flowers in the woodlands, and you may see violets, primroses, cowslips, coltsfoot and the wild arum, with its unusual flower spikes. Look out too for the butterflies, such as the orange tip, which may be resting on the white flowering hedge garlic.

GIRL GUIDES

LOOKING AFTER YOUR PETS

Advice on pet care from the PDSA

Illustrated by Marjorie Owens

Before taking on the responsibility of a pet it is important to think very carefully. A pet animal is not a creature to be picked up on whim, but a living thing which will rely on you for everything it needs, from exercising and grooming if you choose a dog, to cleaning in the case of caged pets.

We all know that a new baby in the family needs love and attention as well as a warm bed and food, and we must also realise that a pet animal needs looking after in very much the same way.

So, if you are thinking of asking your parents for a pet, just stop and think for a while, and talk it over with the rest of the family. If it is going to be your pet, are you prepared to make sure it has the correct amount of food every day, adequate housing and, of course, equally as important, will you spend time with your pet each day? It will look forward to your company and attention almost as much as its dinner! Also discuss with your family what sort of pet you can afford to keep, and if you are thinking of buying a dog, remember he will need a good collar and lead, inoculations, a lot of space, and a licence.

DOG

We will start with dogs as they are the most popular pets in Britain today. Most people have a favourite breed, but when making **your** choice remember three things:—

1. The larger the dog, the more exercise and food it will need.
2. Some coats are far more trouble to look after than others.
3. A very small or very large dog is likely to be more expensive than other dogs.

Dogs may be acquired from many sources but always ask the advice of an expert to make sure that the dog you choose is healthy. Once you have acquired a puppy it is vital to have it inoculated. Your local vet will be able to advise you about these injections.

To keep a dog healthy, the correct diet is important. Your dog will need one balanced meal per day, and fresh water should be available at all times. He will also need plenty of exercise if he is to stay healthy. Dogs must never be allowed to run about unsupervised, and should always be kept on a lead in areas where traffic or farm animals are around. It is most important that a dog wears a collar all the time. This should have details of your name and address attached, in case the dog ever gets lost. There's no need to teach your dog elaborate tricks, but it is essential that he be well-behaved. Plenty of books are available on training and lists of dog-training classes can usually be obtained from your local authority.

All dogs benefit from regular grooming, to keep their coats in tip-top condition. A good quality metal comb with smooth even teeth or a styling comb should be used.

CAT

Cats are the second most popular pets in Britain and this is probably because they are affectionate, yet make very few demands upon their owners. Most pet cats are short-haired and have no pedigree—these types are easiest to look after.

Cats, as well as dogs, have to be inoculated, and these injections can be carried out by your local vet. The PDSA does not give inoculations as it only treats animals which are sick or injured. At about 5-6 months it is a good idea to have your cat neutered, as this will prevent any unwanted kittens. Cats are easy to feed, needing just two meals a day when fully grown. These meals should be mainly meat, and should be supplemented by a saucer of milk in the morning. Of course, a supply of water should always be available. Cats like a warm, secure place to sleep and a sturdy cardboard box, lined with newspaper and an old woollen garment, is ideal. Daily grooming for long-haired and once or twice weekly for short-haired cats is a necessity if your pet is to remain in the best of health. Finally, please remember to ensure that your cat wears a collar and name tag which gives your name and address. The collar should have an elastic insert to allow a means of escape if the cat gets caught up in a branch or bush.

RABBIT

I NEED...

correct feeding
a supply of fresh water
good housing
clean bedding
companionship and exercise
general observation of my health

As rabbits can be kept outside all the time in quite a small garden they are ideal pets for people who live in small houses.

Hutches should be cleaned out weekly and any damp or dirty bedding removed and replaced as necessary. The floor should be covered with sawdust and then with a generous layer of straw.

A fully-grown rabbit should be given two meals a day. These should consist of bran mash, or good quality mixed rabbit food, which can be bought in pet stores, and good quality hay. Rabbits also need green foods (cabbage and cauliflower leaves are ideal) and fresh water should always be available.

Rabbits need exercise, and this can be provided by a wire-netting enclosure, as large as possible and supported by strong stakes driven into the ground about four feet apart. This can then be moved around the garden, always remembering to give shelter from the sun. Alternatively a rabbit can run free if the garden is safe.

Rabbits also enjoy human companionship and look forward to their owners' daily attention.

HAMSTER

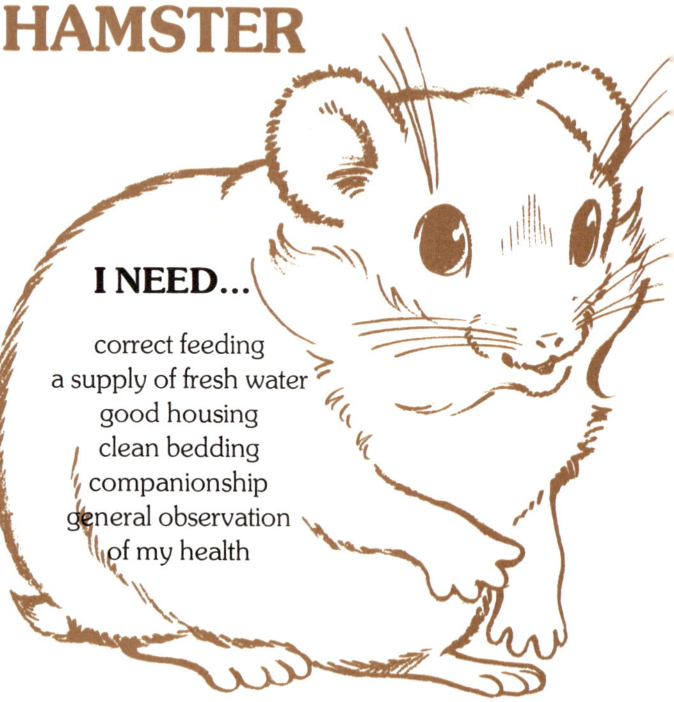

I NEED...

correct feeding
a supply of fresh water
good housing
clean bedding
companionship
general observation
of my health

Golden Hamsters were introduced into this country from Europe and Asia about 25 years ago and they make delightful pets.

Their main diet should consist of good quality mixed hamster food, as well as small quantities of other foods, such as puppy meal, scraps of egg, fish, bacon rind, porridge and other cereals, sometimes mixed with a little milk or gravy. Fresh green food or portions of root vegetables should be given regularly.

For drinking, milk or water should always be available and a few drops of cod-liver oil may be added to the milk occasionally.

A hamster's cage should be kept in a warm room and a small sleeping box should be placed in one corner. A layer of sawdust is most suitable for the floor, while a small amount of hay or wood-wool makes a comfy bed. The whole cage need only be cleaned once a week, provided the damp corner is attended to daily.

A hamster loves to play and some budgerigar toys, or even an ordinary piece of paper, will give him hours of fun. It is also advisable to furnish the cage with a small section of the branch of a fruit tree, complete with bark for the hamster to nibble on, which will help to prevent his teeth becoming overgrown.

This information on dogs, cats, rabbits and hamsters only provides basic guidelines. If you really do want a pet, it is a very good idea to borrow or buy books on the type of animal you want, and then study them hard before taking on the responsibility of a pet. Remember, a pet is a living creature just like you, and needs love and companionship just as much as food and shelter.

THE BEST KEPT VILLAGE
THE BROWNIES OF GREENTHORN STEEPLE WERE VERY BUSY AT PACK MEETING...
THERE'S A FROWN COW ON THE MOON!
THERE'S A BROWN COW ON THE MOOR!
WHAT DID THE SEMAPHORE MESSAGE SAY, JANE?
BOTHER, WE'RE ALWAYS MIXING UP B AND F!
THAT'S A NEAT PARCEL, SALLY. IF YOU USE A SLIP KNOT, YOUR STRING WON'T SLIP.
THANKS FOR THE TIP, BROWN OWL.
THE PIXIES WERE PRACTISING SKIPPING...
MARY AT THE COTTAGE DOOR.
ONE, TWO, THREE, FOUR...
...AND THE IMPS WERE WALKING ON PLANTPOTS!
COME ON, BETTY.
YOU'RE DOING FINE!
OH... HELP... OH...
DON'T FALL ON THE TOADSTOOL!
SOON IT WAS TIME FOR THE CEREMONY THE BROWNIES LOVED BEST OF ALL—
PACK EVERYTHING AWAY NOW, BROWNIES. IT'S POW-WOW TIME.
MAY I TAKE MY BOOK OF PRESSED FLOWERS HOME FOR MY FAMILY TO SEE, PLEASE?
YES, OF COURSE!
BROWNIES, I HAVE SOME EXCITING NEWS. THE PARISH COUNCIL HAS DECIDED TO ENTER THE 'BEST KEPT VILLAGE' CONTEST THIS YEAR!

EVERYONE WAS EAGER TO HELP...
WE'LL PICK UP ALL THE LITTER.
WE'LL WEED THE GARDENS!
LET'S THINK OF SOMETHING EXTRA SPECIAL FOR THE PACK TO DO.
SO EVERYONE PUT THEIR THINKING CAPS ON AND...
LET'S PLANT SOME BULBS BY THE ROAD-SIDE AS YOU ENTER THE VILLAGE.
THEY WILL REALLY WELCOME THE JUDGES.
WHAT A LOVELY IDEA WE COULD USE OUR POCKET MONEY TO BUY THE BULBS.
WE CAN EVEN RAID THE RAINY DAY FUND FOR A REALLY FINE DISPLAY.
AND SO BEGAN A VERY BUSY TIME FOR THE BROWNIES...
OH DEAR, MORE USED BUS TICKETS!
NEVER MIND, WE'LL SOON PICK THEM UP!
THE COUNCIL HAVE PROMISED TO PUT A NEW LITTER BIN THERE TOMORROW.
THEY ALL ENJOYED LENDING A HAND.
I DO LIKE YOUR WISHING WELL!
MY, HOW TIDY MY GARDEN LOOKS.
LET'S MAKE A WISH- BUT NOT OUT LOUD, OR IT WON'T COME TRUE!
MEANWHILE THE ELVES WERE BUSY PLANTING THEIR BULBS...
MAKE SURE THEY ARE PLANTED DEEP ENOUGH.
MAY I LOOK AT THE PLAN AGAIN?
WHY, CAN'T YOU SPELL?
...IN A VERY SPECIAL WAY...
CAN WE HAVE THE SNOWDROPS AND CROCUSES NOW, PLEASE?
I HOPE WE WON'T MAKE ANY MISTAKES!
CARRY ON BROWNIES, YOU'RE DOING FINE!

IN THE WEEKS THAT FOLLOWED THE BROWNIES KEPT A WATCHFUL EYE ON THEIR BULBS AND CONTINUED TO LEND-A-HAND.
THANK YOU, BROWNIES, MY FENCE LOOKS A TREAT NOW!
WE LOVE PAINTING, DON'T WE, JANE?
OH, YES!
IS THIS YOUR DOG, MR. SMITH? I THINK HE'S HURT HIS PAW.
HE'S GOT A THORN IN IT.
ONCE AGAIN THE BROWNIES COME TO THE RESCUE...
THERE YOU ARE, TINKER, THE THORN'S OUT NOW. IT WON'T HURT ANY MORE. I'LL BANDAGE IT UP TO KEEP IT CLEAN.
YOU ARE KIND CHILDREN. I DO HOPE WE WIN THE COMPETITION AFTER ALL YOUR HARD WORK.
ON THE DAY OF THE JUDGING...
THE BROWNIES OF GREENTHORN STEEPLE
WELCOME YOU
WHAT A DELIGHTFUL SURPRISE!
MOST ORIGINAL!
I LOOK FORWARD TO SEEING THIS VILLAGE!
THE JUDGES WERE SO IMPRESSED BY THE VILLAGE THAT...
I HAVE NO HESITATION IN AWARDING THE SILVER CUP TO GREENTHORNE STEEPLE... AND TO THE BROWNIES IN PARTICULAR FOR ALL THEIR HARD WORK!
DOESN'T THE SIGN LOOK LOVELY?
WINNER OF BEST KEPT VILLAGE COMPETITION
YES, AND WE MUST TRY TO KEEP IT THERE NEXT YEAR!
IF ALL THE RUBBISH WE PICK UP, OUR LITTLE VILLAGE WILL KEEP THE CUP!

Crafty Ideas

Try your hand at making these super models, using Copydex adhesive.

BIRD ON A NEST

You will need: a piece of tree bark, straw, grape pips, a small pine cone, beech mast with stalk still attached, a few dried flowers, Copydex adhesive.

1.
Break off the centre spike from the top of the cone.

2.
Arrange the straw into a nest on top of the bark, using plenty of Copydex to fix it into position.

3.
Stick the cone into the centre of the nest with its scales pointing upwards, and leave until the Copydex is quite dry.

4.
Stick the beech mast head onto the top of the cone.

5.
Add the tail and wings made from dried flowers, then leave until the adhesive is quite dry.

6.
Finally stick two small grape pips on the head to make the eyes.

UNTIDY WOODLAND SPRITE

You could make this as a Six mascot, if you are in the Sprites!

You will need: a piece of tree bark, a pine cone, an acorn cup and an acorn, 4 pieces of twig about 5cm long, two small pieces of dried grass, a chestnut seed case, fruit pips (eg. grape seeds), and Copydex adhesive.

1.
Break the top central spike from the cone.

2.
Look for a small, natural hollow in the bark and fill with Copydex adhesive.

3.
Place the bottom of the cone in the hollow and leave to dry.

4.
Stick the acorn into the acorn cup and leave to dry.

5.
Stick the two small pieces of dried grass to the ends of the two twigs to make hands, then leave to dry.

6.
When the glue is dry, stick the acorn and its cup well into the top of the cone where the spike has been removed.

7.
Wedge the legs between the body and the bark, securing with Copydex.

8.
Fix the twig arms to the body by sticking them along two of the scales of the cone.

9.
Stick a piece of chestnut seed case to the top of the acorn head to make the hair.

10.
Now add grape-pip eyes, nose and mouth.

Butterfly and Insect Box

You will need: a cardboard box—lid about 40cm × 23cm, egg shells, feathers, acorn cups, leaves, chestnut seed cases, twigs, catkins, dried leaves and petals, beech mast, conifer cones, apple stalks, pebbles, pips from apples or oranges, 'Clingfilm' film wrap and Copydex adhesive.

The bodies can be made from pieces of chestnut seed cases, beech mast, small cones, pebbles, catkins, etc.

The wings can be made with leaves, feathers, pieces of egg shell, étc.

Legs and antennae can be made from twigs, apple stalks, etc.

The eyes can be made from apple pips, grape pips, small seeds, etc.

Experiment with your materials to make different sorts of insects —pretty ones, unusual ones, frightening ones.

Stick the insects and butterflies to the box lid with Copydex. When it is quite dry cut a piece of Clingfilm about 57cm × 23cm. Be careful as it crushes easily. Cover the top of the box with Clingfilm, folding the edges down underneath the box.

All photos by courtesy of Copydex (Tom Biro)

Standing Bird

You will need: a wine-bottle cork, 2 pieces of twig about 4 cm long, an acorn cup with the stalk still attached, a small pine cone, some Copydex adhesive, a few feathers and two orange pips.

1.
Cover the end of the two twigs with Copydex. Now push them into the pine cone, wedging them between the scales. Leave to dry.

2.
Cut off a piece of cork 2 cm high.

3.
Make two holes in the top of the cork with a small pair of scissors (take care when doing this).

4.
Put some Copydex on the ends of the twigs, then push them into the holes. This helps to keep the bird rigid.

5.
Spread some Copydex around the edge of the acorn cup, then place on top of the cone.

6.
Add a long feather to the back for the tail, small feathers for the wings and two orange pips for eyes. Glue them all in place with Copydex adhesive.

CHINA

A special Minicone, designed for you by JOHN RYAN

Those of you who own a set of Brownie Minicones* will already know what fun they are. You simply cut them out and glue them up to make a lovely set of Brownie dolls from six different countries. They are all slightly different sizes so they all fit snugly inside each other.

Now John Ryan, the artist, has drawn another Minicone especially for the Brownie Annual. This time it is a Chinese Brownie, with her pretty green and yellow uniform.

It would be a shame to cut up your annual, so why not trace over the doll and make one of your own out of thin cardboard? That way you can have the fun of colouring her in, too.

Just trace the whole outline carefully onto the cardboard, then draw in the features, etc., and colour in your doll with coloured pencils or felt tip pens. Now cut out the figure carefully—being sure not to cut off the glue tab—and fold it over, as shown in the diagram. Glue the two cut ends together (it helps to hold them in place with a paperclip while the glue is drying) and your Chinese Brownie doll is complete!

If you do have your own set of Minicones, this one will fit nicely over the top of the biggest one in the set.

*Brownie Minicones are available from Guide shops and by mail order from our trading centre at Broadheath. Ask Brown Owl about ordering them.

BROWNIES IN CHINA

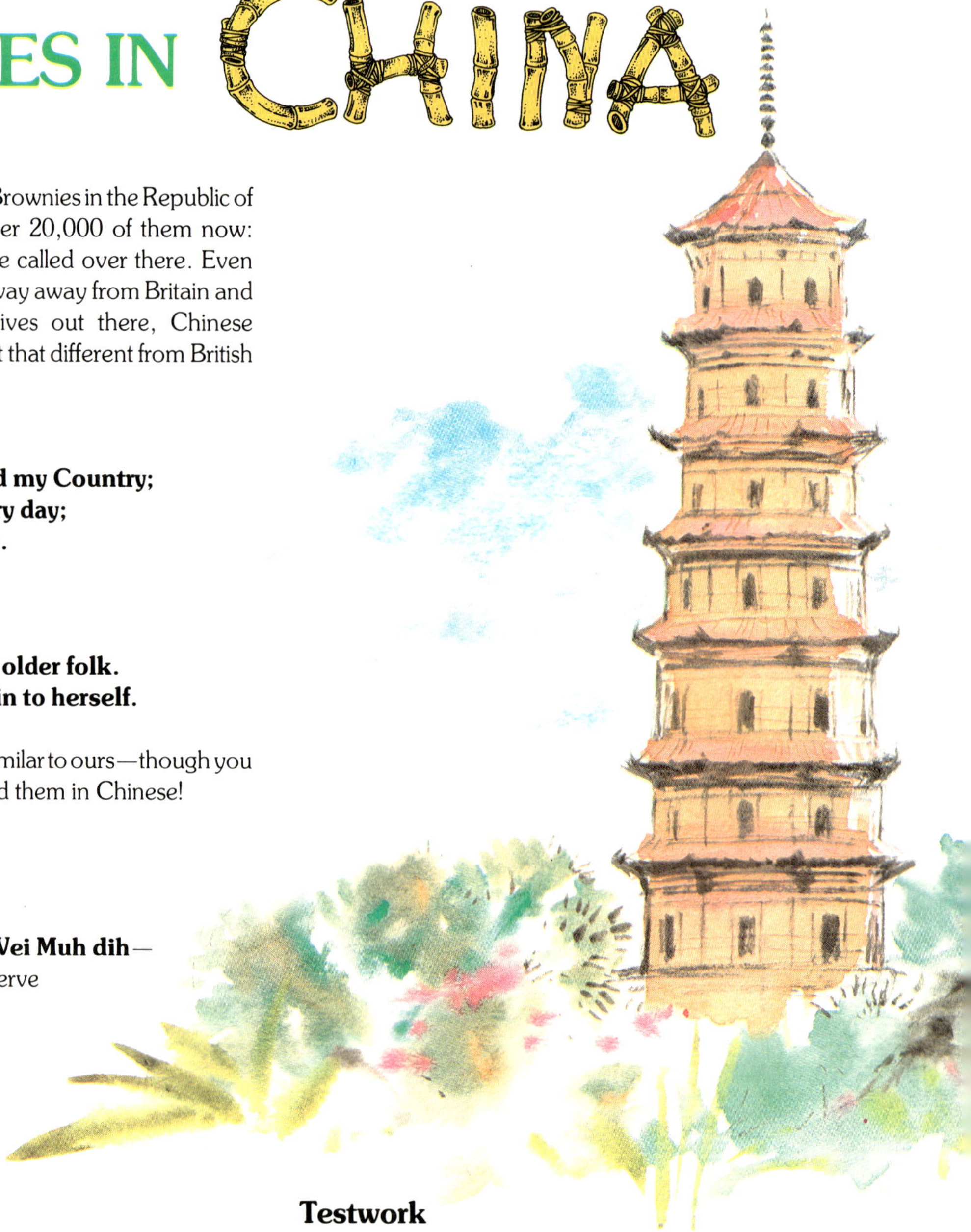

Did you know that there are Brownies in the Republic of China? There are in fact over 20,000 of them now: 'Brownie Scouts', as they are called over there. Even though China is a very long way away from Britain and people live very different lives out there, Chinese Brownie Scouts are really not that different from British ones. Here is their Promise:

I promise to do my best:
To do my duty to God and my Country;
To help other people every day;
Especially those at home.

And here is their Law:

A Brownie gives in to the older folk.
A Brownie does not give in to herself.

Even their mottoes are very similar to ours—though you wouldn't think so if you heard them in Chinese!

Joen bey—Be prepared
ryh Shyng Yi Shann—
Do a good turn daily
ren Sheng Yii Fwu Wuh Wei Muh dih—
The greatest aim in life is to serve

Even though they are called Brownie Scouts, however, Chinese Brownies do not wear a brown dress like you. Instead, they wear an unusual green dress and cap, with yellow trimmings and tie. They have a very unusual badge, too—a frog, shown against a background in the shape of a flower. The colour of the badge varies according to the progress the Brownie has made with her tests. She is given a silver 'pin' when she passes her first tests, then a gold one and finally, as she grows older and passes more difficult tests, a green one.

Testwork

The Brownie Scouts of China take tests which are very similar to yours. They learn about all sorts of things for their 'Golden Bar' tests—for example, their national flag (shown here) and their local customs. They have to know how to wash the dishes—and the chopsticks!—properly, and how to grow and look after plants. They learn how to prepare fresh fruit and serve a fresh fruit salad, and how to keep their silver, gold or green badges bright and shiny.

Good turns

Brownies in China do many good turns around their homes, and love to help their parents look after younger brothers and sisters. They often act out little plays to entertain other people, sometimes making their own costumes for the play too. They cut out collars and cuffs from cardboard to transform their dressing-up clothes into all sorts of magical outfits. Have you ever tried this?

Two games Chinese Brownies like to play

1.
LAME CHICKEN. Each of the teams (Sixes) has ten sticks (or slippers, or anything else suitable). These are placed 10 to 12 inches apart like the rungs of a ladder—one row in front of each team, and several feet away from the players. The first Brownie in each Six is the 'lame chicken'; she must hop over the sticks without touching them. After hopping over the last stick, she reaches down and picks it up, then hops back with it and places it at the beginning again. The next Brownie then becomes the 'lame chicken'.
A Brownie is disqualified if she touches both feet on the ground at the same time or touches a stick when hopping.

2.
WATER SPRITE. Two lines of Brownies face one another, 20 to 60 feet apart. Between the two lines, the Water Sprite stands—the place in the middle is a river. The Water Sprite beckons to one of the Brownies to leave the bank and cross the river. She then covers her eyes and counts to ten. The Brownie to whom she signalled now signals to another Brownie on the opposite bank while the Water Sprite has her eyes covered. The two Brownies then try to change places while the Water Sprite tries to catch one of them. When she succeeds, the Brownie she catches becomes the next Water Sprite.

Language

Most people in the Republic of China speak Mandarin. Here are three greetings a Chinese Brownie Scout might use:

good morning 早安! tsao an (pronounced: jow arn)

thank you 謝!謝! hsieh hsieh (pronounced: zay zay)

goodbye 再見! tsai chien (pronounced: chai jen)

Things to do now:

1.
Could you make a cardboard copy of the Chinese flag, shown here, and make a flagpole for it?

2.
Have you ever eaten a Chinese meal? Ask your mother about Chop Suey, Chow Mein and other Chinese dishes.

WILD FLOWERS IN THE CITY

by Ann Pinder

Illustrated by Pat Harby

In the city plants appear in the most unlikely places, and not always at ground level. Many are found sprouting from rooftops or from cracks halfway up walls – places where they seemingly have little soil in which to put down roots.

The seeds of these city-lovers arrive at their destinations by a variety of means: they are transported by wind, by birds (in their droppings), they sometimes steal lifts on the feet and clothes of passers-by or cling to the fur of wild animals and pets.

Stinging Nettle

STINGING NETTLE

Most people avoid contact with this painful plant, but if it weren't for the nettle, there would be few butterflies in town gardens and parks. Some of the most colourful of our butterflies —the Red Admiral, Peacock and Small Tortoiseshell—only lay their eggs on nettles.

Examine the leaves closely in early summer, especially those of nettles growing in open, sunny places, and you may well see caterpillars feeding together amid a mass of silken threads. They use these threads for drawing up the edges of the leaves, building a safe shelter for themselves.

BUDDLEIA

In the 1890s this shrub was introduced to British gardens from China, and it took so well to English life that now it has spread to the wild, and can be seen beside roads and railway lines, and peeping out of cracks in old buildings.

When it blooms in July its honey-scented nectar attracts a variety of wildlife, from the butterflies which have given it its nickname of 'Butterfly Bush' to the bumble bees, honey bees, and hover flies, all of which do a valuable job in pollinating flowers as they fly from bloom to bloom. Ladybirds visit the buddleia in search of greenfly, and tiny spiders spin their webs among the flowers.

DANDELION

Pick a dandelion and a sticky white liquid comes out of its stem. This is a very special kind of rubber solution, produced to seal up cuts from infection and so protect the plant while healing takes place—a kind of natural Elastoplast!

During the Second World War, when supplies of rubber to Russia were cut off, their scientists experimented to see if dandelion rubber could be produced commercially. How successful they were we don't know. The plant is useful in other ways: its leaves are cooked as a vegetable and brewed for a refreshing tea.

DAISY

Children have been making daisy-chains for years, but in the Middle Ages the daisy was made into an ointment which knights rubbed on their bumps and bruises to soothe away the pain. So it was called 'bruisewort'. Its original name, however, was coined by the Saxons. They noticed how the long white florets always closed over the central yellow disc at night—just like an eyelid closes over the human eye during sleep. So they called it 'the day's eye', thus, daisy.

GREATER PLANTAIN

Sprouting from cracks in the pavements, the plantain seems to be always in danger of being trampled underfoot. But its rosette of leaves hugs the ground so closely that little damage is done by a carelessly-placed foot. Indeed, it is an actual advantage, since its hard seeds are picked up on the soles of shoes and are carried along to grow into new plants.

Buddleia

Dandelion

Greater Plantain

Its seeds, clinging to the feet of ship's passengers, have found their way to Australia and America. The natives there came to believe that the plantain sprang up wherever white men walked and so they called the plant 'white man's foot'.

ROSEBAY WILLOW HERB

Londoners call this plant 'bomb-weed', because in the Second World War a great many of these plants grew up on bomb sites, brightening up these areas with their tall red-mauve spikes. When the rosebay released their plumed seeds into the air, it was as though the city was experiencing Autumn snow showers.

Nowadays it is often found growing on railway embankments. The trains blow the seeds along, distributing them further up the track.

SHEPHERD'S PURSE

Though related to the cabbage, this pavement plant in no way resembles it, being small-leaved, with tiny white flowers. It has the most attractive seed cases—miniature hearts which look just like the purses medieval peasants hung from a string at the waist. This similarity to the medieval purse gave the plant its name, a particularly apt one, since the seeds in each capsule are golden and round, just like tiny coins.

BRAMBLE

On a patch of waste ground there is almost always a bramble (or black-berry), climbing over other plants by using the hooked spikes along its stems. To us it means an Autumn harvest of blackberries for apple pies; to birds and small mammals it is a source of food.

There is a legend told about the blackberry. This recounts how Satan, thrown out of Heaven, landed on Earth in a blackberry bush. He was so angry with the prickly plant that ever since, on the anniversary of his humiliation (October 10th), he has visited every bush to breathe on it and spoil its fruit. Country folk say it is unlucky to pick blackberries after this date.

SCARLET PIMPERNEL

This little flower makes an excellent clock because it is so punctual in its habits, opening its petals around 8 am and closing them again in the early afternoon; this habit has given it the nickname of 'John-go-to-bed-at-noon'. It has another unusual name, too: 'the poor man's weather glass'. This refers to its habit of always closing its petals when it feels dampness in the air. Normally its flowers are red, but look out for the blue or white blooms too.

RED CLOVER

Have you ever looked for a four-leaf clover? They are said to be lucky. Generally, though, clover leaves are made up of three separate leaflets, (like the Guide trefoil), those of the red clover having a horseshoe-shaped white marking.

This is Britain's earliest flowering clover. It blooms from mid-May onwards, and though found by the wayside in towns, it is specially grown in the country by hive-keepers who have discovered that the bees make an excellent honey from the nectar.

Easy Cooking

Fruit Kebabs.

1 banana, 1 pear, 1 orange, 1 peach, 2 plums.
(these fruits are ideal but any selection will do)
2oz. sugar, ½ teaspoon ground cinnamon

Cut the fruit into bite sized pieces and roll in sugar and cinnamon. Thread the pieces onto skewers, wrap each kebab in foil and bake in a hot oven (400°F mark 6 for 20 minutes, or cook over an open fire for 10 minutes. Unwrap and serve.

Sunset Salad.

2 tomatoes, 1 large orange,
1 small onion, lettuce leaves,
french dressing (3 parts olive oil to 1 part vinegar, salt and pepper)
(or buy it ready-made)

Slice the orange, tomato and onion thinly, and arrange them on the lettuce leaves. Pour over the french dressing.

Tomato and Orange Soup

1 tin tomato juice, 1 tin orange juice,
a few drops of Worcester sauce, orange slices.

Mix together the contents of both tins and add a few drops of Worcester Sauce to taste. Serve hot or cold with a slice of orange floating in each bowl.

Eggs in Nests.

2 eggs, 1 large potato, grated cheese,
butter, salt and pepper.

Bake the potatoes, (350°F mark 4) for 1½ hours or until soft. Scoop out the inside and mash with butter, salt and pepper. Put back into the potato shells making a hollow in the centre with the back of a spoon. Break an egg into each hollow, cover with grated cheese and bake (400°F mark 6) for 15 minutes.

Lemony cream.

1 small carton double cream, whipped,
3 tablespoons lemon curd, 1 egg white

Whip the egg white until stiff. Mix the lemon curd into the cream and fold in the egg white. Serve chilled with a biscuit.

METRIC CONVERSIONS

(approximate)

1oz	= 25g
2oz	= 50g
$2\frac{1}{2}$oz	= 65g
4oz	= 100g
6oz	= 150g
½pt	= ¼litre
325°F	= 160°C
350°F	= 180°C
400°F	= 200°C
8in	= 20cm

Banana Milk-shake.

Blend in a blender, or whisk well with a fork, or hand whisk, 1 banana, ½ pint milk and 1 tablespoon thin honey. Serve chilled, with a scoop of ice-cream on top and with a straw!

Brownies!

2½ oz. butter, 2oz. plain chocolate, 6oz. caster sugar, 2½ oz. self-raising flour, ¼ teaspoon salt, 2 eggs, beaten, ½ teaspoon vanilla essence, 2oz. walnuts, chopped.

Melt the butter and chocolate in a bowl over hot water and add the sugar. To the flour add salt, the chocolate mixture, eggs, vanilla essence, and walnuts. Beat until smooth and pour into an 8" square cake tin which you have greased and floured.

Bake for 35-40 minutes in a moderate oven (350°F mark 4) until the mixture is risen and firm to touch.

Leave in the tin to cool, then cut into fingers to serve.

Jelly Oranges.

4 oranges, 1 packet orange jelly.

Cut the oranges in half and squeeze out juice. Mix juice with water to make up the orange jelly, following the directions on the packet. Remove pith from orange halves and fill with warm jelly. Leave to set, then cut into quarters.

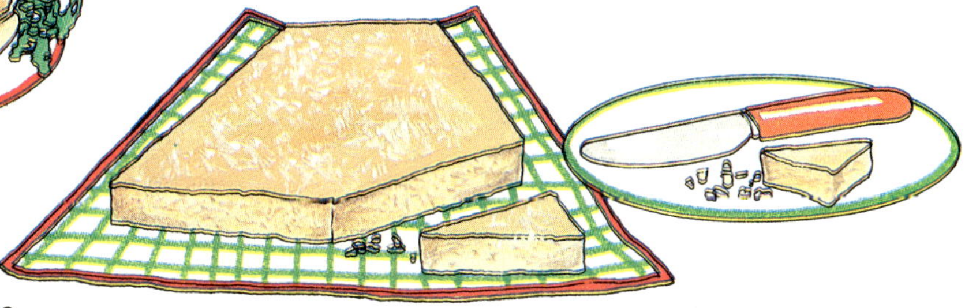

Cheese and Raisin Potato Cakes.

6oz. boiled mashed potato, 2oz. fresh breadcrumbs, 4oz. grated cheese, 1oz. chopped raisins, 1 egg, salt and pepper

Mix together the potato, breadcrumbs, cheese and raisins. Add salt and pepper to taste, then mix in the beaten egg. Form into little cakes and fry until golden brown.

Shortbread.

6oz. flour, 4oz. butter, 2oz. sugar.

Add the sugar to the flour. Beat the butter to soften it and add the flour/sugar mixture gradually. Put into a shallow baking tin and bake (325°F mark 3) until firm and golden.

Turn out and sprinkle with sugar.

Look at Summer

Summer is a good time for spotting all kinds of birds. Look for swifts and swallows whirling and wheeling in the sky, and the yellowhammers and whitethroats perched on the hedgerows. You may be lucky enough to see a Green Woodpecker too, or a Little Owl at dusk. Look out for the summer flowers, for instance, buttercups and daisies, poppies in the wheat fields, purple thistles, clover and the clustered white flowers of the hedge parsley. But beware this plant's large relative, the giant hogweed, which can blister your skin if you touch it. The hedgerows too are bright with the colours of bindweed, bramble blossoms and wild roses. You may see hedgehogs, lizards, or any of the other small animals of our fields and woodlands, and there are also many butterflies and insects to spot, as they busily search for food.

ATARAH The Pied Piper of Rossendale

by Hilda Young

Everyone knows about the Pied Piper of Hamelin. Now month by month, year by year, more people are learning about another Pied Piper, Atarah Ben-Tovim, who, in her home on Rossendale moors at Haslingden and at her many concerts throughout the country, is giving children and their parents a new 'fun' way of looking at music.

And Atarah's concerts are fun... I've been to one myself so I know! They're a mixture of clowning, pantomime, merriment, early music, light classical music, jazz and rock and pop. Whatever you want, Atarah has got it, together with her zany band, all talented musicians but also sometimes turning the stage into chaos with their animal antics! All this is woven together by Atarah herself, bubbling over with such great enthusiasm that even if you have only the slightest interest in music you just can't help laughing and wanting to learn more about everything.

Pre-school, infants, juniors and seniors; all are welcome. Atarah wants everyone to join in, listening, singing, clapping, and entering a light-hearted quiz to win a prize! You won't get bored because all the pieces are short, Atarah insists upon that! And all the time she chats away happily to you, joking and giving you lots of fascinating information... you might even get a chance to play the drums!

If, after attending one of her concerts, you feel you would like to learn more, you can go along to Atarah's Concert Centre, at Haslingden, Lancashire, and try out any instrument you like. Atarah knows that some-one who just can't hit the right note on the piano, might have ideal fingers for a trumpet, and if you like noise, the percussion room could be just the place for you!

At the Centre there are different rooms for the different instrument families... percussion, brass, string, keyboards, woodwinds, rock and jazz, and a quiet room just to enjoy music. There is also a music library, a canteen, practice rooms, recital rooms and a social 'get-together' room.

So, go and meet Atarah, either in concert or at her home on the hills. She'll welcome you with musical arms if you are lucky enough to attend one of her open days. She'll help you and listen to what you have to say and above all, she'll make music fun and give you a hobby or interest which will last you a lifetime!

For the way she has pioneered music for pleasure for thousands of children, Atarah was awarded an MBE in the 1980 New Year Honours.

Atarah makes learning music fun for this group of boys and girls.

inside the PDSA

The People's Dispensary for Sick Animals was founded in 1917 by Maria Dickin, to provide free treatment for sick and injured animals whose owners could not afford private veterinary fees. In those days the standard of living in many cities was very poor. Many people who owned animals, either as pets or as working animals, could not afford to pay money for treatment when their animals became sick or had an accident. So when Maria Dickin started the PDSA she knew that she was helping the poor people as well as their animals.

She opened the first dispensary in a cellar in Whitechapel in the East End of London and within five years she had a total of seven dispensaries in London.

One of the early dispensaries in London's East End.

Today, treatment of sick and injured animals is still provided free by the PDSA to those who cannot afford private fees. There are now 58 Animal Treatment Centres throughout the country, which are staffed by 120 Veterinary Officers and 160 Animal Treatment Centre Assistants. Many Centres nowadays have X-ray and laboratory equipment, a preparation room and operating theatre, and wards in which animals can recover after operations.

Each year three-quarters of a million animals are treated by the PDSA. A large number of these are owned by old-age pensioners who rely on their pets for companionship.

Many families would not be complete without the opportunity to love and care for a pet, and it is for this reason that the PDSA not only treats animals but also encourages people, especially children, to take a responsible attitude towards pet ownership. It provides informative literature on how to look after all the popular pets, supplies films free on loan and gives talks to schools and other organisations.

The PDSA runs a 'Busy Bees' Club, (which has its own magazine) for children between the ages of 5 and 11 years. There are six editions of the magazine each year and they offer pet-care information, animal stories, items about the PDSA and Busy Bees' activities, competitions, puzzles and animal posters. Busy Bees' members work together in groups, or 'Hives', to raise funds for the PDSA, and so help sick animals. The Busy Bees are part of a larger club called the PDSA Club. This, too, has its own magazine, **Club News,** which has the same format as **Busy Bees' News,** but is designed to appeal to a readership of all ages.

The PDSA is supported entirely by voluntary contributions. It receives no state or local authority aid.

If you would like further details about the PDSA or the Clubs, write to:

The People's Dispensary
for Sick Animals,
PDSA House,
South Street,
Dorking,
Surrey,
RH4 2LB.

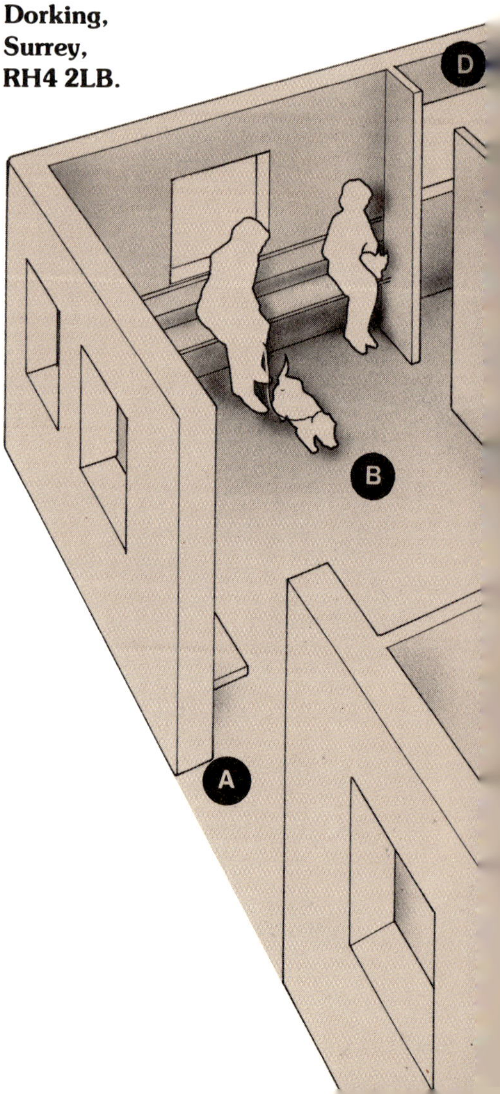

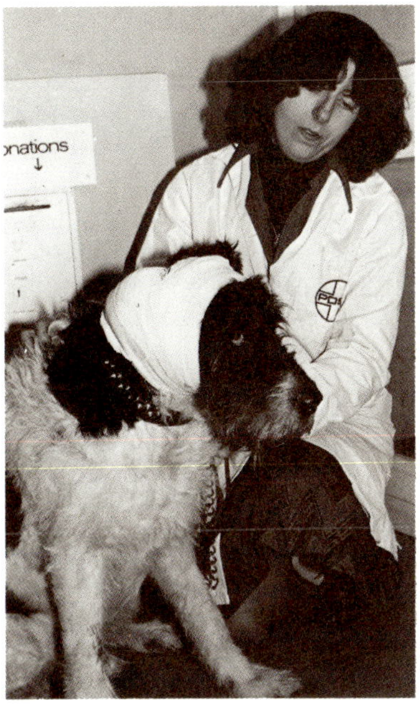

A sad-eyed patient recovering from an ear operation at the PDSA in Hendon, London.

A Public Entrance

B Waiting room for owners and their pets

C Receptionist in her office

D Combined X-ray and third consulting room

E Darkroom for developing X-ray film

F Staff rest room

G1 Sterilizer for preparing surgical instruments

G2 Minor surgery and animal preparation room

H Staff showers and toilets

I Operating theatre with hydraulic table, lights and anaesthetic machine

J Ward with cages for cats and dogs recovering from operations

K Office for Veterinary staff

L Rear entrance porch

M Store for cleaning materials

N Laboratory for diagnostic tests

O Store room for medicines

P Two consulting rooms

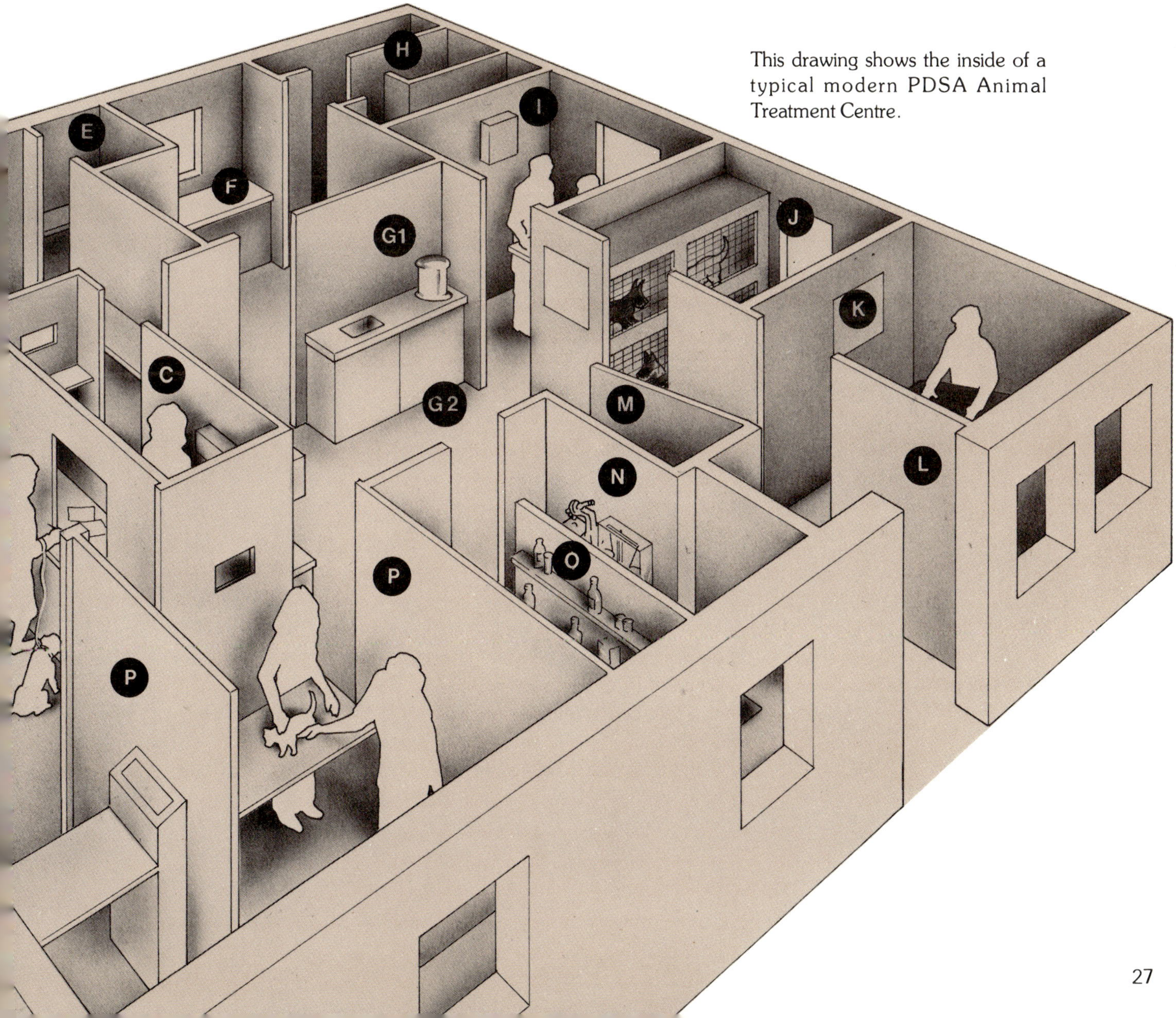

This drawing shows the inside of a typical modern PDSA Animal Treatment Centre.

GIRL GUIDES

IN ALL JEST

by Fiona Lawson

The Brownie Jester badge is always very popular, because it is such fun to work for. You can sing, dance, play a musical instrument, or entertain people in various other ways.

Do you know the meaning of the word 'jester'? The dictionary tells us that a jester was 'a professional entertainer at Court, etc.' In the Middle Ages, every king, and most noblemen, had their own jester. He lived in the household of his master and was paid a regular wage like all the other servants, but his particular job was to keep his master from feeling miserable by making him laugh. He had to have a constant supply of new jokes, songs and tricks on hand at all times, ready to do his cheering-up job. Do you think you could make people laugh whenever they asked you to? It would be hard work, wouldn't it?

The court jester wore a very odd costume, which made people laugh just to look at him. He was a well-known figure in medieval days as he strolled around in his multi-coloured tunic, tight trousers, and hood with bells a-jangling on top of it. He usually carried his 'bauble' around with him—a short stick with a jester's head carved in wood on the top.

Court jesters not only sang songs and told jokes, however, they also talked about things which no one else dared to: telling wicked stories about other people, for example. They were allowed to do this only because it made the king laugh. In France, Louis XIV's jester used to stand behind the royal throne making rude remarks about famous men at Court. These men used to bribe the jester with money to keep quiet!

Some jesters became quite famous. There is a famous one in Shakespeare's play 'As You Like It' called Touchstone, and Henry I's jester, Rahere, was the founder of the very old and well respected London hospital Saint Bartholomew's. Charles I was the last British king to keep a Court jester.

You don't need to do quite as many things as the Court jesters did to pass your Jester Badge, but you will have to choose three ways to entertain people from the list given in the syllabus. One of the suggestions is:

'Dress up and act or mime, or use puppets, to illustrate a well-known story or an event from history'.

If you choose to try this section, and decide to put on a puppet show, you will probably want to make a puppet theatre first. There are lots of different ways of doing this; here is one suggestion which is quite easy to make up if you follow the step-by-step instructions. (You may need a little help from an adult.)

You will need

A cardboard box with a flap top (the kind used for packets of biscuits, chocolate bars, sauce bottles etc., not less than 35cm long. Most shops or supermarkets will give you one, if you ask.

* **Patterned wallpaper or wrapping paper, coloured food wrappers, coloured tissue and paper doilies.**
* **Old buttons and beads.**
* **Strong thread.**
* **Small pieces of material for curtains and floor coverings.**
* **Thin card for the backdrops.**
* **A piece of 0.5cm dowel rod, about 2.5cm longer than the box.**
* **Copydex adhesive and Plasticine.**

Instructions

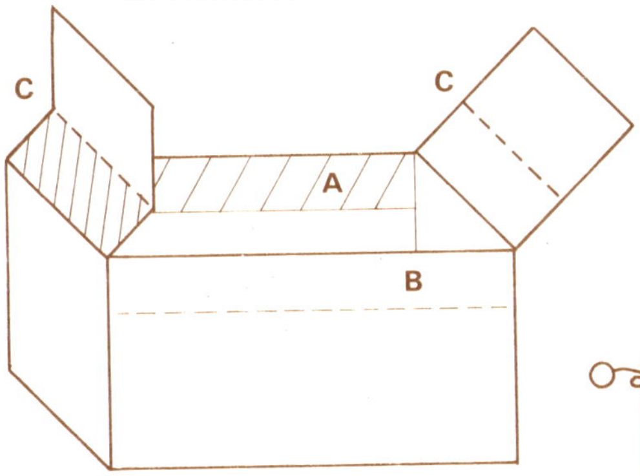

1

1.
Stick the long flaps (A and B) inside the box. Turn back the short flaps 2.5cm from the fold (C), and stick them down to make the panels on either side of the stage.

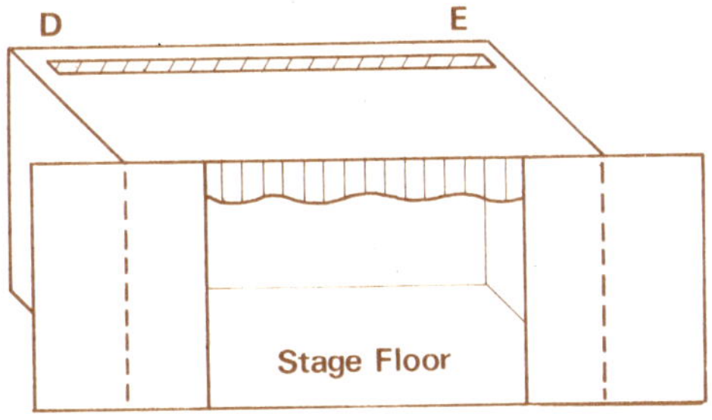

2

2.
Cut a slit from D to E, 2cm wide and 2cm from the back and sides of the box, to make a slot for inserting the backdrops.

3.
Line the box with light-coloured paper. Decorate the front panels with attractive wallpaper, using Copydex adhesive to stick it down. Make a pelmet (from wallpaper) for above the front of the stage to hide the curtain fittings.

4.
Make a hole on each side of the box, 1.5cm from the top and front, to take the dowel rod.

5.
Cut out two curtains from your pieces of material, remembering to allow plenty of material for them to hang in 'folds'. If the edges look ragged, turn over a small hem and sew or stick it down.

6.
To affix the curtains to the dowel rod, oversew the top edge at 1cm intervals all the way along.

7.
Insert the dowel rod (with the curtains attached) into the box, and put a blob of Plasticine on each protruding end. Stick a two-hole button near each of the holes.

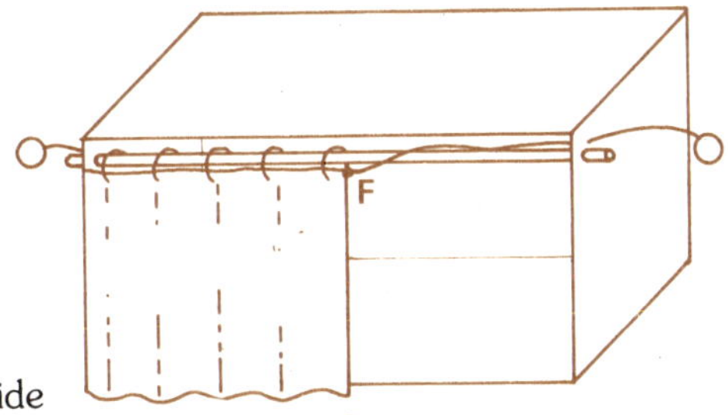

8

8.
To open/close each curtain, take a piece of thread three times the length of the box and knot it firmly at point F.

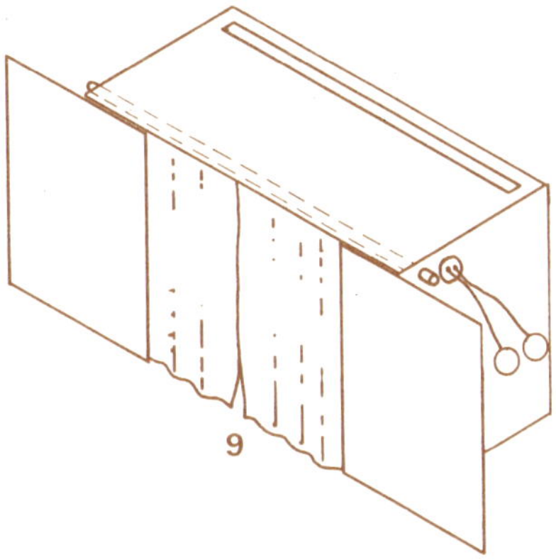

9

9.
Thread one end to the left of the stage, through the side of the box and through one hole in the button, and the other in the same way to the right. Tie a bead onto the end of each thread to prevent the threads being pulled right through. Now you can open and close your curtains by pulling the threads at the sides.

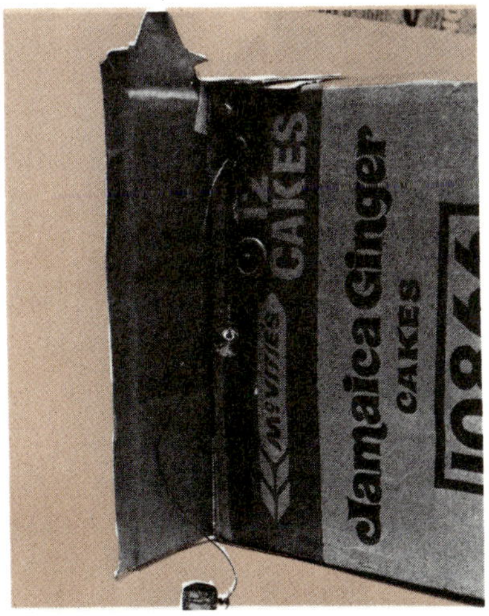

10.
Cut out a piece of material to fit the floor of your stage. Spare backdrops can be made from a collage of coloured pictures cut out of magazines, etc. (See photograph). The decorative heading ('Theatre Royal') in our photograph was cut out of card and glued on with Copydex.

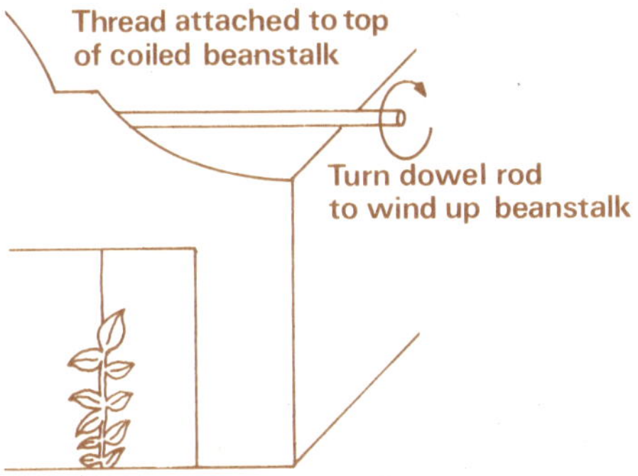

A 'GROWING' BEANSTALK

You can also make extra pieces of scenery to suit the particular story you are telling. For example: for 'Jack And The Beanstalk', a beanstalk can be made to grow by fastening one end of a coiled, green tissue to the stage floor and raising it from above by pulling a thread (see diagram).

Once you have decided on the story you are going to perform, you can start to make the cast. You will need to make moveable puppets to act out the story, but sometimes it is helpful to have a few cardboard characters standing in the background of the stage. These 'extras' are made quite simply by drawing the shape you want (eg. lion, queen, herald—see photograph) on a piece of fairly stiff white card, and colouring it in. Fix flaps to the back so that the characters will stand up (see diagram).

Here is an idea from Geoffrey Hemming for a super puppet.

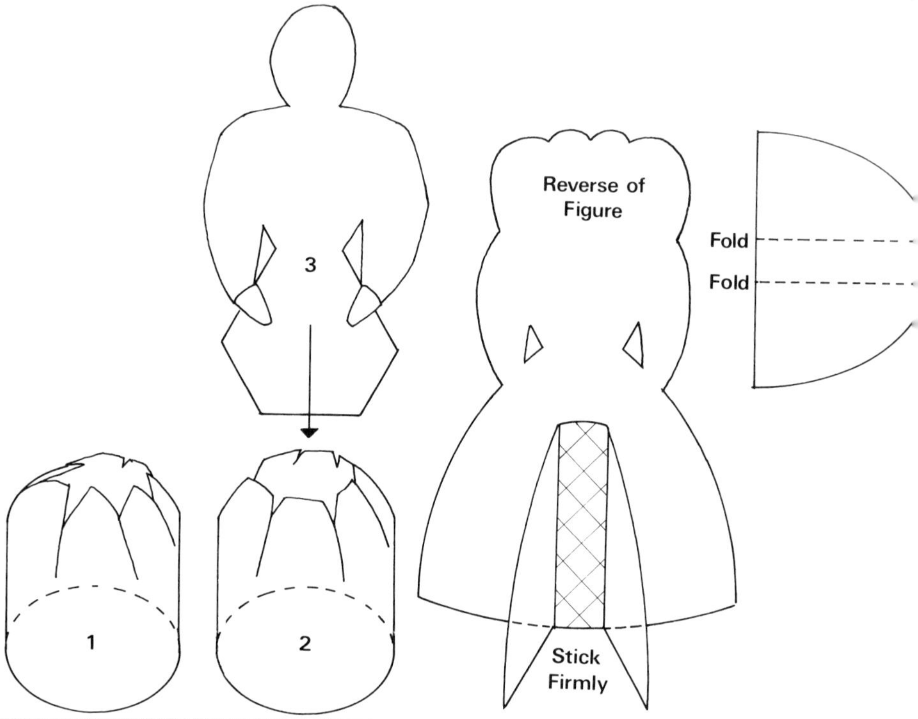

FINGER PUPPET WITCH

Mother Windflew is a finger puppet witch who is easily made and great fun to play with.
To make her, collect:
A narrow cardboard tube
Straw
Thin cardboard
Paints
Glue

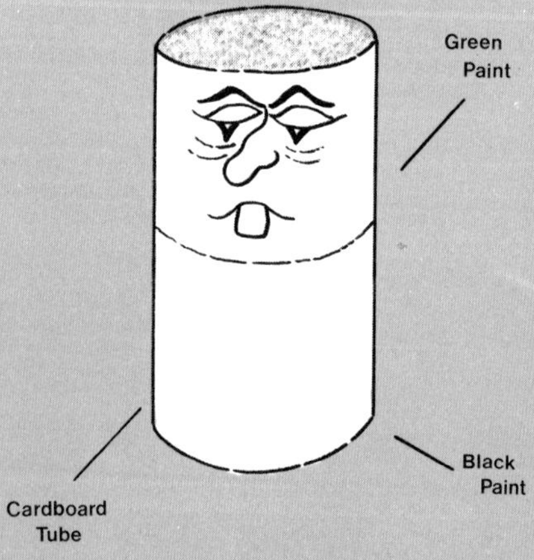

DIAGRAM 1

Cut a length of cardboard tube about 8cm long. Paint the top half green and the bottom half black. When the green paint has dried, paint in the face, with a fine brush, in black.

DIAGRAM 2

Cut the straw into short lengths and glue them around the top of the tube for hair. If you don't have any straw, wool will serve the same purpose.

DIAGRAM 3

Bend a piece of thin cardboard into a cone shape. Glue the joins together and round off the bottom. Now glue the cone to the centre of a cardboard circle. Paint it black, and you have the witch's hat.

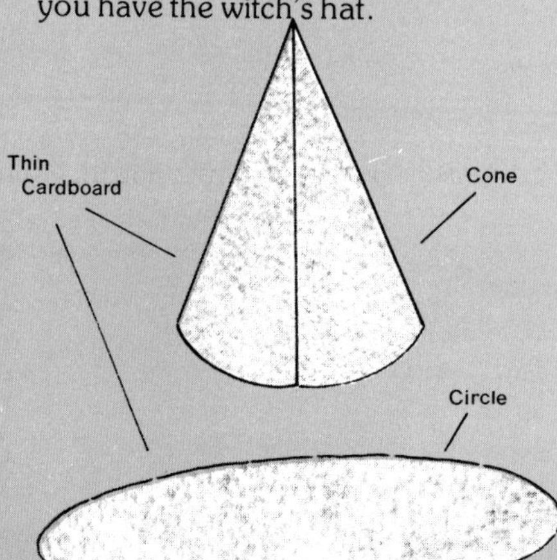

DIAGRAM 4

When the paint has dried, glue the hat over the top of the tube. Slip the tube onto your index finger. Use your thumb and middle fingers for the puppet's arms and Mother Windflew is all set to give her first bewitching performance!

Of course there are lots of different puppets you can make. A particularly useful book for young puppeteers is Ladybird's 'How to make puppets'.

Whatever you decide to do, enjoy working for your Jester Badge!

JOANNA joins the BROWNIES

by Susan Guy

Illustrated by Tim Marwood

For as long as she could remember, Joanna had wanted to become a Brownie. She lived with her grandmother in a cottage overlooking the field where the Brownies met in the summertime. Every Tuesday she had watched them playing and working. Every Tuesday she wished she could join them. They always seemed to have such fun.

Now she was seven. The great day had arrived and she was at last going to join the Brownies, not in the playing field, but in the Village Hall, because it was still winter. Would she become a Gnome, an Elf or a Kelpie? She didn't know. Her best friend Julie had been a Brownie for two months. Julie was a Gnome, but Joanna secretly hoped she would be a Kelpie. Joanna's daddy worked in Scotland, and Joanna knew that Kelpies came from Scotland. She wanted to have something special to tell him when he came home, for this time he was bringing a new wife with him.

Joanna's mother had died when Joanna was two, and since then she had lived with her grandmother. Her father joined them when he had leave from his job in Scotland.

It seemed a long time until Julie came to collect her. At last there was a knock at the door, and there was Julie, with a broad grin on her face, looking very smart in her new uniform. Oh, how Joanna wished she could wear her uniform! Her grandmother had given it to her as a birthday present two days before, and now it was hanging up in the cupboard waiting for the day when she would make her Promise.

Together the two friends walked down the road to the Village Hall, or rather Julie walked, while Joanna skipped along beside her and never stopped asking questions. Did Julie know which Six she'd be in? What games would they play? Was anyone else joining the Brownies that evening? What was Brown Owl like?

The last question was soon answered. At the door to meet them was a lady with one of the kindest faces Joanna had ever seen. "Welcome to the Brownie Pack! You must be Joanna. I'm afraid we haven't room for you in Julie's Six, but the Kelpies are longing to welcome you to their Six. Would you like to go with Julie tonight and join the Kelpies next week when you will know everyone, or would you like to become a Kelpie straight away?"

"Straight away, please," said Joanna, beaming.

Brown Owl took her by the hand and led her over to a group of smiling girls in one corner of the hall. Two of them she knew from school, but the others were strangers. Not for long, though! She soon learnt their names, and they showed her the Kelpies' treasures and explained what happened in the Brownie Ring.

How the evening flew by! First they played some games, then they had the Brownie Ring. Joanna was able to join in the song as she had already learnt it from Julie. What fun they had throwing their Brownie pennies into the Wishing Pond. Everyone who managed it could have a wish. Oh, how hard Joanna wished she would like the mother her father was bringing home. After more games, and after Brown Owl had helped Joanna make a Good Turn Mouse to take home to remind her to do at least one good turn a day, it was time for Pow-Wow.

Brown Owl told them that in eight weeks' time she was going to be married! There was great excitement among the Brownies. Could they come to the wedding? Should they wear their Brownie Uniforms? Could they make a Guard of Honour like the Brownies whose picture they had seen in 'The Brownie' Magazine?

Brown Owl said she had hoped they would want to be a Guard of Honour; yes, of course they would be wearing their Brownie Uniforms, and she hoped by then Joanna would have made her Promise and she would be able to join them too.

Then came the bombshell. "There's only one problem," said Brown Owl. "I don't suppose any of you know someone who would like to become a Brownie Guider?"

Various Brownies made various suggestions, but they were all people who had been asked before and couldn't manage it.

It was a rather subdued Joanna who returned home that night. She had so much wanted to become a Brownie. Now that she was able to join the Pack it looked as if there would be no Pack to belong to.

Four weeks passed. Joanna was ready to make her Promise. She asked Brown Owl whether they could wait another week for the Promise Ceremony. Then her father and new mother would be home and she did want them to be there for that special day. So the ceremony was fixed for the next week.

Imagine Joanna's excitement as she dressed in her smart new uniform! But underneath the excitement she was sad. They still had not found a new Brownie Guider, and Brown Owl was leaving in two weeks' time. She went downstairs to show her father, mother and grandmother the uniform. Her father had come home that week, bringing with him his new wife, and she was quite the nicest person Joanna could have imagined. Added to this they had told her that they were going to settle in the village and live with her and grandmother. The wish she had made her first night at Brownies had come true, but not the one she had made every week since then.

"My, how smart you look!" said her new mother. "You remind me of my Brownie Pack, back in Scotland."

"Were you a Brownie too?" said Joanna.

"No, I was a Brownie Guider, and I didn't know how much I was going to miss the Brownies until I saw you in your Uniform."

"Oh," said Joanna, "my wish has come true. We must go at once." Taking her mother by the hand she rushed her off to the Village Hall and to Brown Owl.

"I've found her, I've found her!" said Joanna breathlessly.

"Found who?" said a mystified Brownie Guider.

"Why, our new Brown Owl!" said Joanna.

A quarter of an hour later, when all the explanations were over and grandmother and father had arrived, a very happy and proud Joanna made her Promise.

GIRL GUIDES

HOW DOES YOUR GARDEN GROW?

Nothing looks nicer than a mass of spring flowers in a window box. You don't have to wait till the spring to start your garden though! Anyone can grow a colourful display of flowers indoors during the bleak winter months. Hyacinths are easiest to grow, but all sorts of other bulbs can be forced into early flower: tulips, daffodils and crocuses, for example. It's easy when you know how!

All bulbs contain a tiny flower, leaves and a stem, as well as a supply of food to produce a lovely bloom. Before they can flower, however, bulbs need a period of cold. During this period, of about three months, the bulb grows its roots outside and its stem and leaves inside. Later, by bringing the bulb into the warmth and light of the home it can be 'forced' to flower earlier than bulbs planted in the garden.

Always choose top quality bulbs—plump, solid and free from blemishes. The largest size will produce the best results. Hyacinth bulbs should be planted in October or November, daffodil and tulip bulbs in September and October and crocus bulbs in October.

You can grow bulbs in almost any type of container, as long as it is clean and at least twice the depth of the bulb, to give enough room for the roots to grow. Place a few flat stones over any drainage holes to stop the soil leaking out. Then partly fill the container with potting compost (if it has drainage holes) or bulb fibre (if it has no drainage holes).

Next, place the bulbs gently but firmly on top of the compost so that their tops are just below the level of the rim. (When using bulb fibre in bowls without drainage holes, first soak the bulb fibre thoroughly, and then squeeze it out until it stops dripping.) The bulbs should not touch each other or the sides of the pot. A 15cm pot will take 6 tulips or about 15 crocuses. Hyacinths can be potted singly or in groups of 3-5 of the same variety. Daffodils are best planted in groups of 5 or more.

Add more compost or bulb fibre, pressing it firmly with your fingertips to anchor the bulbs, but leaving their

Information and colour photographs by kind permission of the Dutch Bulb Information Desk.

tips exposed and with enough room for watering. Water thoroughly. Now label each container, noting the date planted, the variety and colour.

Your bulbs must be allowed to develop strong roots before they begin to grow upwards, so give them a period of 'cold storage' in the dark for 12 weeks or so. An ideal home for them would be in a dark and airy cellar, garage or outdoor shed. Water them regularly to prevent the soil from drying out, but don't let the soil become waterlogged, and be extra careful in frosty weather that the bulbs don't die of cold.

When your hyacinth sprouts are at least 5cm high move them to a semi-dark area in the home where the temperature does not exceed 60°F (15°C). After a week, move them into full sunlight, and the flowers will bloom in a few weeks.

Daffodils need about 14 weeks 'cold storage' before bringing indoors in mid-January. Daffodils like it cool, and a temperature of 45-50°F (7-10°C) is hot enough until the buds are clearly visible. (Keep the pots near daylight or the leaves will grow too tall.) Then move them into a heated room (about 50°F or 10°C). Just before the buds open, spray some water over them, but when the plants are in bloom less water should be given.

Tulip bulbs also need to be kept in the dark for around 14 weeks. Then bring your pots or bowls into a dark room, no hotter than 60°F (15°C), to permit the stems to lengthen. After 2 or 3 weeks they can be moved into the light, but shade them from direct sun for the first few days by covering them with paper.

Small bulbs like crocus require a cold period of 14-16 weeks before they can be brought into a living room with a temperature of 60-65°F (15-18°C). Shade them from direct sun for a few days, and when the shoots turn green they can be exposed to full light.

Water your bulbs regularly and keep them away from direct heat or draughts. A good tip to make the flowers last longer, is to move the pots to a cooler place during the night.

It's great fun and not at all difficult to grow hyacinths in water. You can buy special glass or plastic containers in florists' shops or garden centres. First drop a bit of charcoal in the clean glass to keep the water sweet. Then fill the glass with water so that it almost, but not quite, touches the base of the bulb where it rests on the curve of the glass or the shelf of the plastic container. Hyacinths grown in water must also be stored in a cool, dark, well-ventilated place in the 12 week root formation period. Remember to top up the water if it falls below the level.

If you want bulbs to flower for Christmas you must buy 'specially prepared' bulbs. These have been specially treated to bloom extra early. They are grown in the same way as other bulbs, but the timing is different. 'Specially prepared' bulbs must be planted in September and brought indoors in the first week of December. They would make super Christmas presents!

succeed with SEEDS!

by Ann Martin

Illustrated by Linda Sandey

Have you ever thought what fun it would be to have your own little garden indoors? All sorts of unlikely things can be grown inside, a few of which are mentioned here. Do you know any others?

Mustard and Cress

You can buy packets of mustard and cress seeds in any garden centre. They are very cheap and easy to grow. Sow them on moist blotting

paper or a piece of thick cloth such as a flannel (but don't use your face cloth!). Keep the cloth damp. After about two weeks your mustard and cress will be ready to cut and make into delicious salads and sandwiches. To add a bit of variety, why not spell out the name of your Six or pack? This is done by carefully sprinkling the mustard and cress onto the moist blotting paper to form the various letters. Then when the seeds grow, you will see the word you have written.

Broad Beans

This is a good way to find out how seeds begin to grow. The process of beginning to grow is known as germination. You will need: blotting paper, a jam jar, a broad bean, water. Roll the blotting paper up so it fits tightly round the inside of the jar. Pour in 30mm of water—this will be soaked up by the blotting paper. Push the bean between the glass and the blotting paper. Watch carefully every day and you will see how a seed grows. Dampen the blotting paper again if necessary. You can also use other big seeds such as peas and sunflower seeds.

Vegetable tops

When your mother is not too busy, ask her if you can have the tops off the vegetables she is cooking for dinner. Place the top in a saucer with a little water. After a few days the top will form roots and begin to grow. A carrot top gives lovely green leaves, try it and see. You can also try to grow the top of a pineapple.

Lentils

While still in the kitchen, ask your mother for some lentils. These will have to be planted in soil and watered every day. Put some soil into a yogurt pot and push the lentils down into the soil. Water well, but don't drown the soil. After a few weeks they will begin to flower. Are there any more things from the kitchen that you think might grow? It's fun to find out!

Fruit pips

Growing plants from fruit is very easy and costs very little. Save the pips from an orange, a lemon, and a grapefruit. Draw a picture of each fruit and stick it to a yogurt pot that is filled with soil. These seeds need a little watering every day and they should be in a warm place with plenty of sunshine. They sometimes take quite a long time to shoot, but when they do they will grow beautiful shiny dark green leaves.

When you have finished eating a peach, instead of throwing the stone away, grow it in a jam jar. This is done by cutting a hole in the lid of the jam jar big enough for the stone to fit into. (Ask your father or mother to do this for you with a pair of sharp scissors.) Fill the jam jar with water until it just touches the stone. In a few weeks roots will appear. Remember to keep the water level so that it just touches the stone.

There are many seeds to be found, both indoors and out. It is a challenge, and lots of fun, to find out if things will grow, and to watch them growing. Always name your seeds, then you will be able to tell at a glance just what it is you are growing. A good idea is to write the name of the seeds on used ice lolly sticks and push them into the soil in the pot.

Look in your Brownie Guide Handbook for more advice on caring for plants.

Would you like to take the Gardener Badge?
Ask Brown Owl about it.

BROWNIE WINNERS

Last year we ran a Competition in The Brownie magazine, asking Brownies to write or draw something for the Brownie Annual. Here is the prizewinning entry, a story written and illustrated by the winner: Kathryn Pollock, aged 9, of Sutton Coldfield, West Midlands. (13th Sutton Coldfield Pack)

THE MAGIC CLOTHESPEGS

There was once a girl called Elizabeth, who was very selfish and horrible. She was eight years old, almost nine. One day, and it was a particularly windy day, Elizabeth was looking out of the window. "Oh, look!" she said to herself, "Mrs McWorthy's washing has nearly fallen off the line. Oh, won't it be fun to see it all covered in mud! Serve her right—the horrible woman!"

However, outside in Elizabeth's garden there was a spare clothespeg who had seen the washing dangling in the mud. Now this peg was no ordinary peg, but a magic peg, and it decided to go to the rescue. The peg flew over the fence and clipped itself onto the washing, and then it lifted itself and the washing up and pegged itself onto the line. Just as the peg had finished pegging itself onto the line, Elizabeth came back to the window. "Who's been rescuing Mrs. McWorthy's washing, I wonder," she said crossly. "I wouldn't have done. It's a silly idea. She should have pegged her washing on properly—it would have been her own fault if it had got all muddy."

That night the peg who had rescued the washing told the other pegs what it had done. "How did you do it?" asked another peg. "We want to know."

"Oh well, I just felt the magic come into me," said the peg, "and I thought it would be a good idea to help someone. Don't you think it was a good idea?"

"Of course it was!" said all the pegs. "There's nothing that can be better! Let's do some more good turns!" Another peg said, "We'll have to keep our eyes and ears open, won't we, if we want to do that."

The next day one peg noticed that there was something hidden in the mud. "I wonder what it is," thought the peg, and went off to see what was in the mud. When he got to the muddy patch where he had seen the 'thing' he scraped about and eventually found a little shoe. "Ugh, it's very messy!" said the peg to himself, "I mustn't spread the dirt around the house, for that won't be helping anyone, will it?" So the peg scraped the mud off on the grass and pulled the shoe along to where all the family's shoes were kept.

Meanwhile another group of pegs had found a baby bird that had fallen out of its nest and hurt its wings.

"What shall we do?" asked one peg. "How should I know?" argued another. "I was only asking," said the first peg again.

"Now don't start arguing you two," said the peg that was in charge. It isn't a very GOOD thing. Now what I think we should do is make a cradle by clipping ourselves together and four of us can lift the bird onto the cradle. Right?" "And then what shall we do?" asked a peg. "We'll fly up to the nest, of course," said the peg in charge.

So that is what they did. Soon they got the baby bird into its nest. Its mother was there and was very grateful for what the pegs had done. "Thank you very much," she said, "I will never forget your kindness."

That night all the pegs gathered together to tell each other what they had done. The biggest pegs, who were in charge, were very pleased with the peg that had rescued the shoe from the mud, and hadn't spread the mud around. "That was very good work," said a head peg. "And so was that turn that a group of pegs did," said another, "to rescue a baby bird." "Well done, all of you," said a leader. "Tomorrow we'll try and do more good turns."

The next day, Elizabeth noticed her baby brother's shoe had been rescued. She wondered who had found it, not that she was bothered because she was only concerned about herself. She went to look out of the window and was trying to spot different kinds of birds when she saw a toy parachute caught in a tall tree at the bottom of the Jamesons' garden. The Jamesons had a boy and a girl. The girl was called Sarah and she was nine, and the boy was called John and he was ten. Sarah was Elizabeth's friend, but Elizabeth hated John, who was really quite a nice boy. She knew that this particular parachute belonged to him. "Oh how funny it will be to see his parachute being torn into tiny bits," thought horrid Elizabeth and she laughed out loud.

However, a peg had noticed the parachute and it decided to rescue it. The peg clipped itself onto the parachute, carefully unhooked itself off the branch, and flew up into the air with it. Then the peg slipped through an open window of the Jamesons' house and popped it on the floor.

Later on Elizabeth saw John Jameson playing with his parachute in the garden. "I wonder who rescued it?" thought Elizabeth rather angrily. "It's a shame, he deserved to have it torn to bits."

However, another peg had discovered a ladybird who had been knocked over, upside down, and couldn't turn herself the other way up. The peg quickly turned her the right way up and the ladybird thanked the peg gratefully. Soon it began to rain. Then it began to pour. Quickly the peg flew to a shelter. At least he was saved from being soaked! But unfortunately lots of things were not and one was right in front of the peg's eyes. It was a poor little begonia growing in a pot. It was soaking and the flowers and leaves were drooping very sadly. The peg dashed to the plant and carried it through an open window and put it down on a table.

Now this particular flower belonged to Elizabeth, who was very fond of flowers, and she was glad when it had been rescued. Elizabeth began to think about all these good turns she had been noticing, and she wondered if she ought to do some too. But she decided that first she would ask her friend Sarah. "Why, of course it's a good idea to do good turns!" said Sarah when she heard. "At Brownies we're supposed to do at least one good turn every day and we do lots of other exciting things as well." "Tell me more about Brownies," said Elizabeth. So Sarah told Elizabeth all about Brownies and what they do. "Could I join Brownies?" asked Elizabeth. "Of course you can," said Sarah. So Elizabeth went to Brownies and enjoyed it very much.

The pegs were thrilled when they heard. "We've changed Elizabeth from a selfish, horrid girl into an unselfish, happy Brownie. That's definitely our best good turn!"

Our first prizewinner, Kathryn

The Runner-up prizewinner was Anne-Marie Troutbeck (aged 9) of the 17th Enfield (Middlesex) Pack, with her lovely drawing of the old rhyme:

I saw eight magpies sitting in a tree,
Four for you and four for me...
One for sorrow, two for mirth,
Three for a wedding, four for a birth.

Here are four of Anne-Marie's drawings:

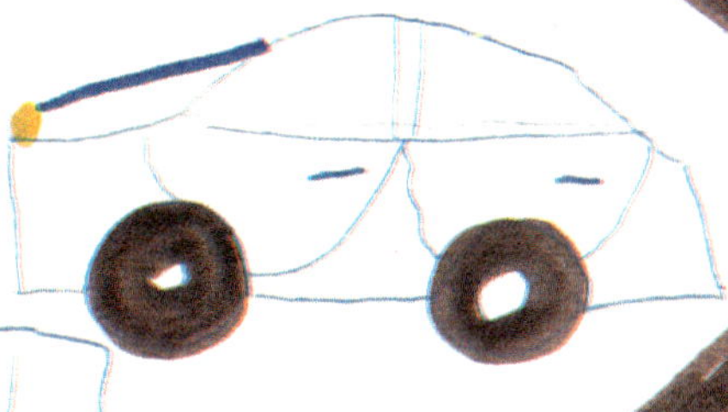

Would you like to see a drawing of yours in next year's Brownie Annual? If so, turn to page 60.

Happy Days...on Pack Holidays

by Susan Guy

Illustrated by Belinda Lyon

Have you ever wanted to have a house of your own to look after? Have you ever played at keeping house, and wished it were real? Well, this is just what happens on a Pack Holiday. For a weekend—or if you are lucky, a week—a hall, or a hut, or a house is transformed into your own home. All sorts of places can become Pack Holiday homes: church halls, village halls, schools, cottages and even Scout and Guide huts. Some counties have their own Pack Holiday Houses and there are four special ones that belong to the Guide Movement: Foxlease in Hampshire, Waddow Hall in Lancashire, Netherurd in Scotland and Broneirion in Wales. Ask your Brownie Guider to tell you about these or your own special County Pack Holiday House.

Pack Holidays are holidays especially for Brownies, not at all like the holidays you have with your family. You go to them with your Brownie Pack and your Brownie Guider. You help with all the important jobs like cooking, cleaning and waiting at table, and you have the fun of helping and planning before you go.

You will have a lot to discuss and decide on in Pow-Wow; what will you do, what would you like to eat, who will go in which group? Very often we choose different groups from our Brownie Sixes.

To make the holiday more fun you may decide to have a theme. This can be taken from a favourite story, such as Winnie the Pooh, The Wombles or Mr. Men, or it could be something that you think up for yourselves. One Pack I know are going to be a circus this year. You change from Elves, Leprechauns and Kelpies, (or whatever Six you normally are), to characters in your chosen theme. If you were Mr. Men you might choose to be Mr. Happys, Mr. Messys and Mr. Sillys. Your Brownie Guider might be Mr. Forgetful, Cook would be Mr. Greedy and First Aider would be Mr. Bump.

Your first job when you arrive will be to unpack. When your bed is made and your things put away, you can help with the rest of the house. There will be charts to put up, homes to find for Pack treasures, the food to unpack and put away. You will also want to explore. Then it will be time to prepare your first meal, eat it and wash up. I expect your Guiders will have thought up something special for you all to do on your first evening —games to play or a special 'Teddy's Sing Song', when everyone brings along their favourite doll or teddy.

By then you will be ready for bed. You will have to take it in turns to wash. You may have basins or showers or, if you are really lucky, you may have a real bath. When every Brownie is clean and in her night clothes there will be a story, prayers and bed.

Will it be camp beds, ordinary beds, or bunk beds? Our Pack's favourite is bunk beds, but everyone always wants to be at the top! Halfway through the holiday we have 'changeover' day when those on the top move to the bottom and those on the bottom move to the top.

Each day you will have a similar timetable: time to get up and go to bed; time for meals and for doing the jobs; prayer time and discussions. After lunch you will have a rest hour when you do something quietly in your bedroom. This is the time to read, to write letters to send home, to keep a diary. You may want to play cards or a game with the Brownie in the bed next to you or you may want to go to sleep.

Each day the groups take on a different job. If you are a cook on the first day, you may become a waitress the next day, then a housemaid, then a messenger. There

are plenty of jobs to be done: cooking, laying tables, waiting at meals, washing up, cleaning the house. There will be plenty of opportunities to put all the things you have learnt at the Brownie meetings to good use. Then there's the shopping to do, the post to collect, flowers to arrange, visitors to welcome, Graces to choose, and prayer times to prepare. You will clean your shoes, make your beds and keep your things tidy. So, you see, you will be very busy!

Does it look as if it is all work at Pack Holiday? The work is fun when you're doing it with all the other Brownies; but there are all sorts of surprising and exciting activities to take part in too: including treasure hunts, trails and picnics. One year Mr. Mischief ran off with our picnic lunches. Luckily he left clues, so that each group could find their own! Perhaps one day you will have sports or a gymkhana with hobby horses you have made, or one afternoon you might have a flower show, 'It's a Knockout', or a fancy dress party. You may go swimming, or visit an interesting place nearby, and you may welcome your parents and friends to your holiday home on Visitors' Day... what a lot you will have to show them!

As well as all this you will want to make presents to take home and you won't want to forget the Brownies who weren't able to come.

All too soon it's the end of the holiday and time to pack. Brownies always leave their holiday homes just a little bit tidier and cleaner than when they came! Perhaps you will want to do a special good turn for your holiday house or for the Pack who will be coming after you.

Has this made YOU want to go on a Pack Holiday? I hope so! And I hope I have given you lots of ideas for Pow-Wow.

Look at Autumn

Autumn is a colourful season, when the leaves on the trees turn to bronze, red and gold, before they flutter to the ground on the wind. There are acorns on the oak trees and brightly coloured berries on the bushes too, but you should always remember that many of them are poisonous to humans. The wild arum, or 'lords and ladies', also has a stalk full of bright red berries, and these are very poisonous indeed. Toadstools thrive in damp conditions underfoot, but you should never touch them. Watch out for squirrels and small mammals, such as shrews and mice, gathering food, and the well-camouflaged partridge under the hedgerow. Other birds to watch for are the pretty goldfinch, the tiny wren, the chaffinch, the nuthatch and the coal tit, with its distinctive black and white head feathers. Someone has carelessly left a milk bottle here: always take **your** litter home with you.

DOT-to-DOT BADGES

by Daphne Pilcher

Join up the dots to find the symbols that appear on various Brownie Interest Badges – then name the Badges!

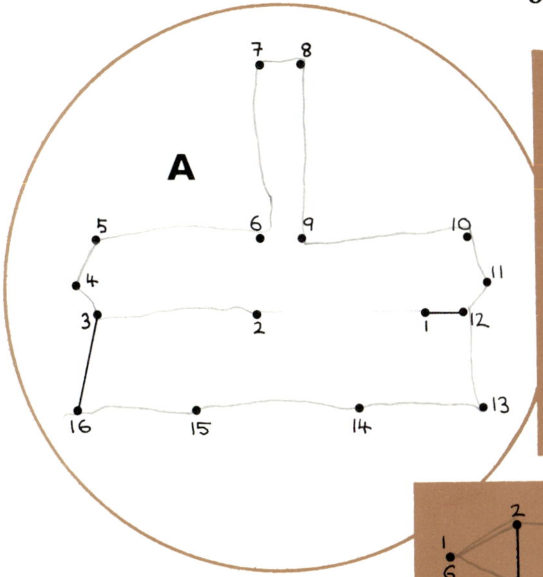

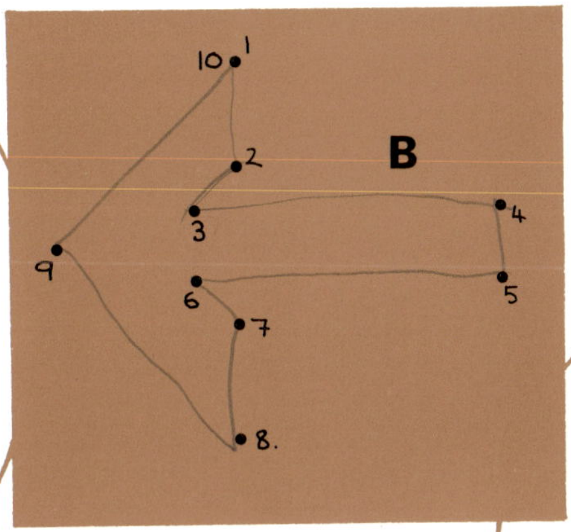

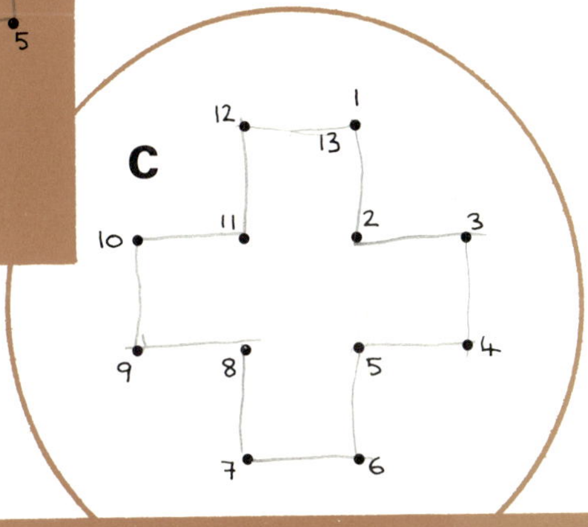

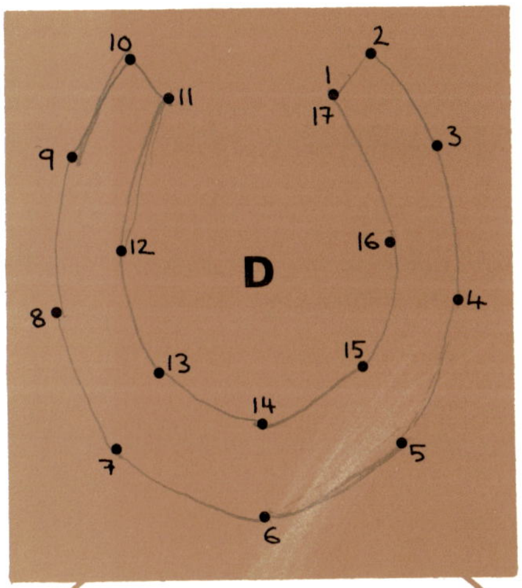

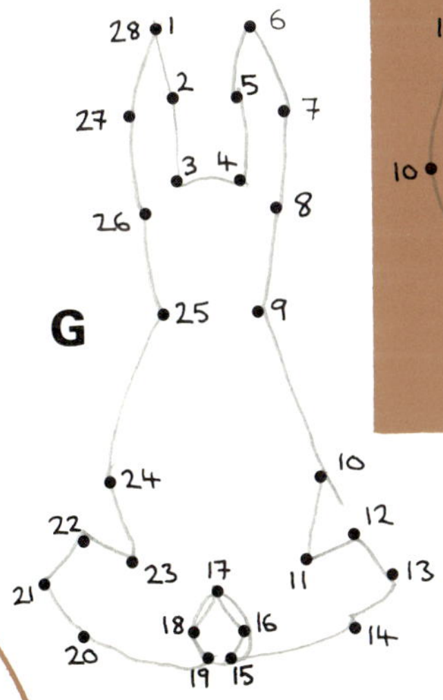

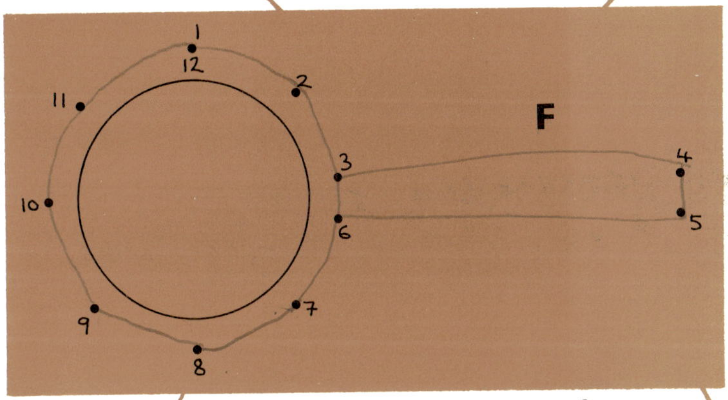

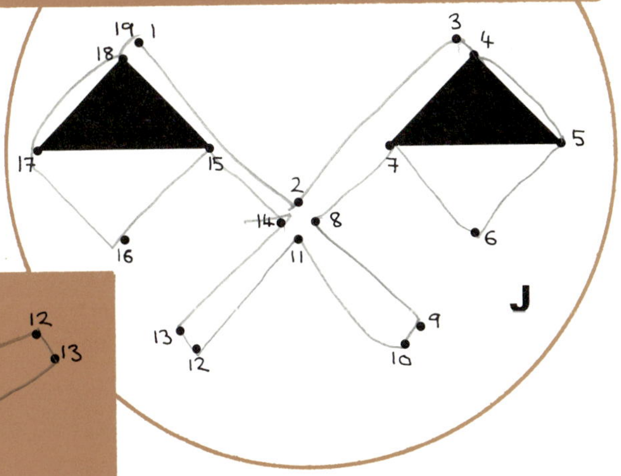

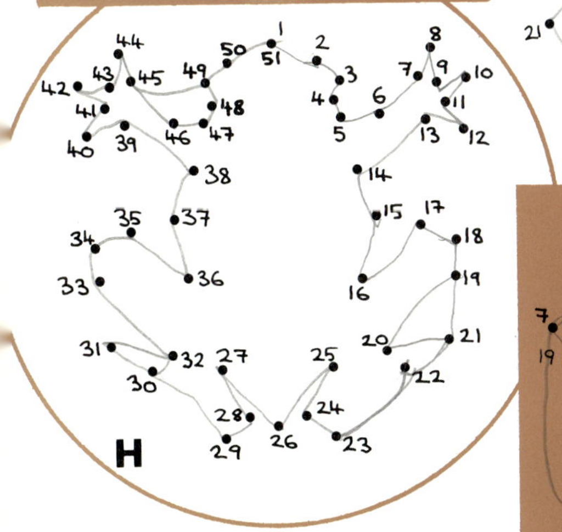

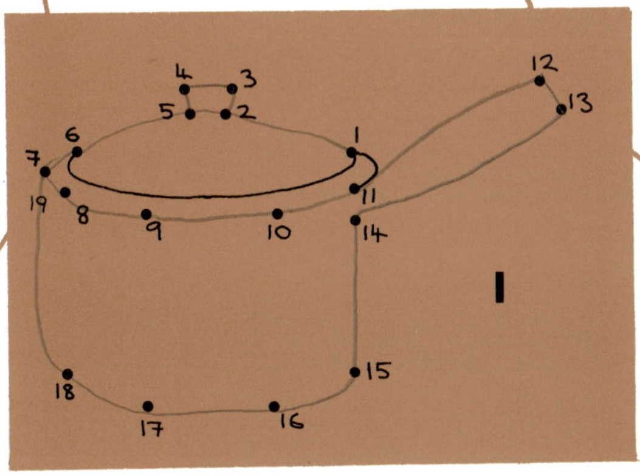

Answers on page 61

Rosebuds

by T. Forbes

I expect most of you know that before Brownies were 'Brownies' they were 'Rosebuds'. The idea was that Rosebuds would grow up to be Roses, but very sensibly those children of long ago pointed out that they did not want to become Roses, they wanted to become Guides... and, what's more, they wanted to do everything the Guides did.

Rosebuds were first mentioned in May 1914 and their uniform was not at all like yours today. They wore dark blue shirts with knitted jerseys and knitted caps or 'tams'. Sometimes they had a white haversack slung over one shoulder, just like the Guides at that time, and sometimes they wore sailor hats. They were allowed to wear pale blue hair ribbons.

A Rosebud saluted with two fingers because she only made two promises:

"On my honour I promise that I will do my best:

1) to do my duty to God and the King:

2) to do a Good Turn for somebody every day."

There were no Brown Owls or Brownie Guiders at first; instead, Guide Patrol Leaders organised Rosebuds because "Captains cannot do all the work themselves". Rosebuds were asked the following question: 'Dubesor a uoyera?" to which every Rosebud who knew anything about anything would answer proudly "Duba mai!" If you do not already know what those words mean (and I'm sure some of you will) you can work it out by starting at the wrong end and working backwards.

What did Rosebuds do? Well, they learned which flags make up the Union Jack and how to fly it, and they practised making many different kinds of knots, besides learning which one to use for what purpose. When the first World War broke out Rosebuds helped by crocheting mittens or scarves for the soldiers, rolling bandages and collecting magazines. They had their own special badge which Agnes Baden-Powell, the Founder's sister, designed for them.

By January 1915 people were beginning to suggest that a better name could be found for Rosebuds, but it had to be "attractive and at the same time dignified". The various suggestions made included names such as 'Buds', 'Bantams', 'Skylarks', and 'Bees', but none of these was

The Rosebud Pack of Much Haddam, Hertfordshire, in 1914.

Brownies at a rally, sometime between 1916 and 1920.

successful. By December 1915 the name 'Brownie' was decided upon, and the Brownies Constitution was approved and printed in full—so, you see, Rosebuds did not last very long as Rosebuds, but 'Brownies' have been reorganised and accepted for years and years. But remember, if you want to count up just how long the Brownies have been in existence you must include the Rosebuds... because they were the very earliest Brownies. After all, what's in a name?

The very attractive metal badge which Rosebuds wore.

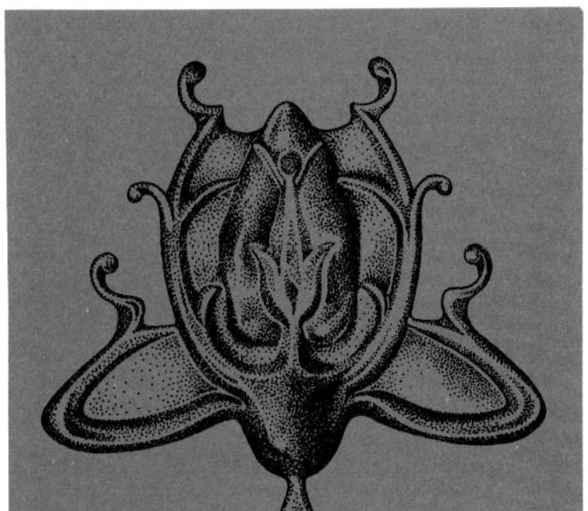

Two smart Brownies of 1916, in navy blue home-made dresses, with brown knitted Tam o'Shanters.

Here is a new song written especially for you by Sue Stevens. Teach it to the other Brownies in your Pack!

Illustrated by Royston Edwards.

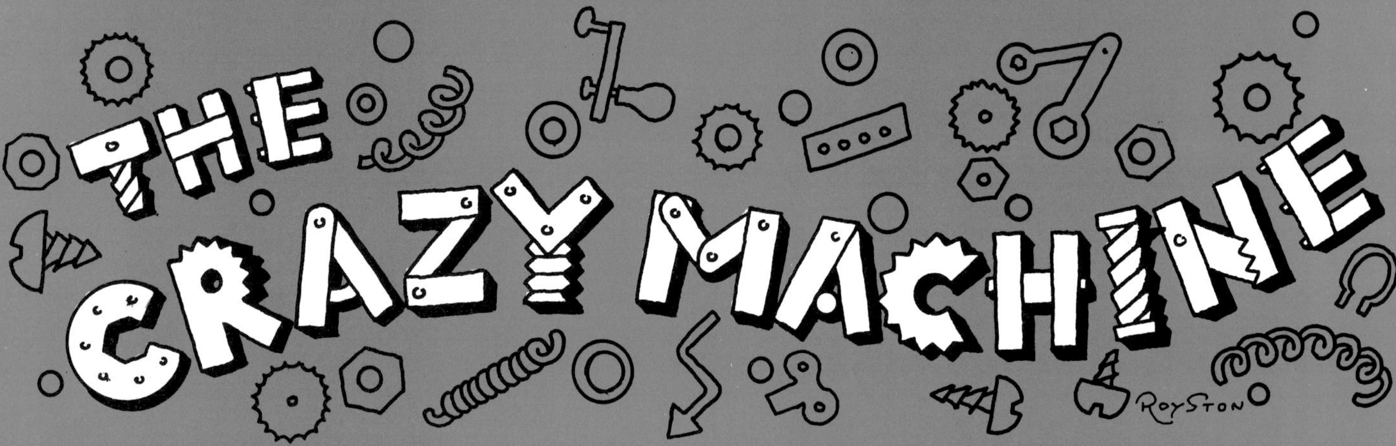

*** This is where you put in your own ideas, with actions to match... sausages... welly boots... lollipops... teddy bears...**

HERE'S HOW YOU CAN TURN YOUR SONG INTO A PACK-SIZED MOVING MACHINE! FIRST, STAND IN A BIG CIRCLE AND FIT THESE ACTIONS TO THE NUMBERS:

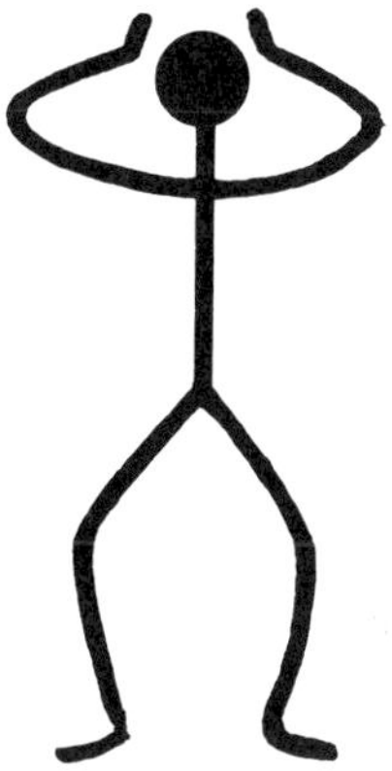

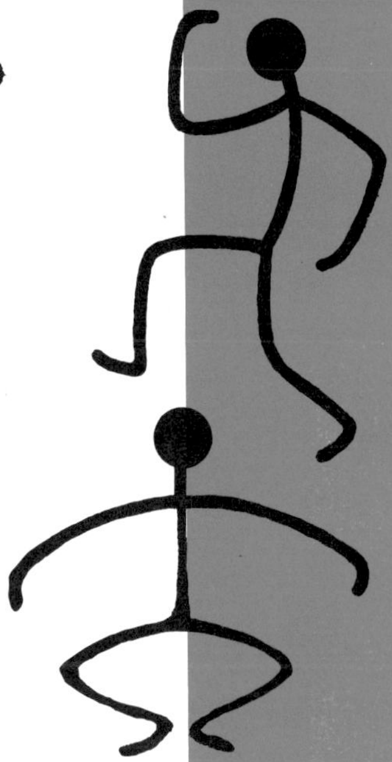

① POINT TO SELF.
② PUT FINGERS TO HEAD.
③ SHAKE WRISTS.
④ MIME BANGING DRUM.
⑤ BEND KNEES.
⑥ PUT FINGERS IN EARS.
⑦ and ⑧ INDICATE LARGE SHAPE.
⑨ and ⑩ INVENT MIME TO SUIT ACTION.
⑪ and ⑫ LOOK AT WATCH.
⑬ to ⑯ TURN TO RIGHT, PUT HANDS ON SHOULDERS OF BROWNIE IN FRONT, AND RUN EIGHT STEPS TO THE RIGHT. THEN YOU TURN TOWARDS THE MIDDLE AND START AGAIN - MAKING SOMETHING DIFFERENT WITH YOUR MACHINE!

PUZZLE PAGE

By Phyllis Mead

SUITCASE PUZZLE

Dinah has packed her suitcase ready to go away on Pack Holiday. Can you work out what she has put in her case? Perhaps you can think of some things which she has forgotten.

SIX EMBLEM CROSSWORD

Do you know the names of all the different Sixes you could have in your Brownie Pack? Fill in their names on the crossword.

Your Brownie Handbook will help you to spell the difficult names.

Brownie Friends Badge Puzzle

Did you know that there are Brownies in over 80 countries throughout the world? Here are nine badges worn by some of our Brownie friends in the North, South, East and West. Can you work out the names of their countries, which have been jumbled up? This puzzle will help you to pass the Friendship challenge for your Highway Badge. Ask your Brownie Guider to show you pictures of Brownies from these countries and find out what they are called.

Answers on page 61

Strange, but True!

by Fiona Lawson

Illustrated by Lynn Breeze

You might not believe some of these funny facts — but they're all true...

The largest jigsaw in the world is called the 'Festival of Britain' and it has 40,000 pieces.

The smallest record in the world is a recording of God Save the King, made in 1924. It measures less than 5cm in diameter.

The oldest magazine in the world is Old Moore's Almanack, which has been published every year since 1697.

A San Francisco man changed his name to Vladimir Zzzzzzabakov so that he could be the last person in the 'phone book.

The smallest book in the world measures 2.1mm by 2.1mm and is a copy of Three Blind Mice, published in Scotland in 1978.

There is a river E in Inverness-shire and an O brook in Devon.

The commonest surname in Britain today is Smith.

The shortest place names in Britain are Ae (in Dumfriesshire), Oa (on the island of Islay), and Bu (on the island of Orkney).

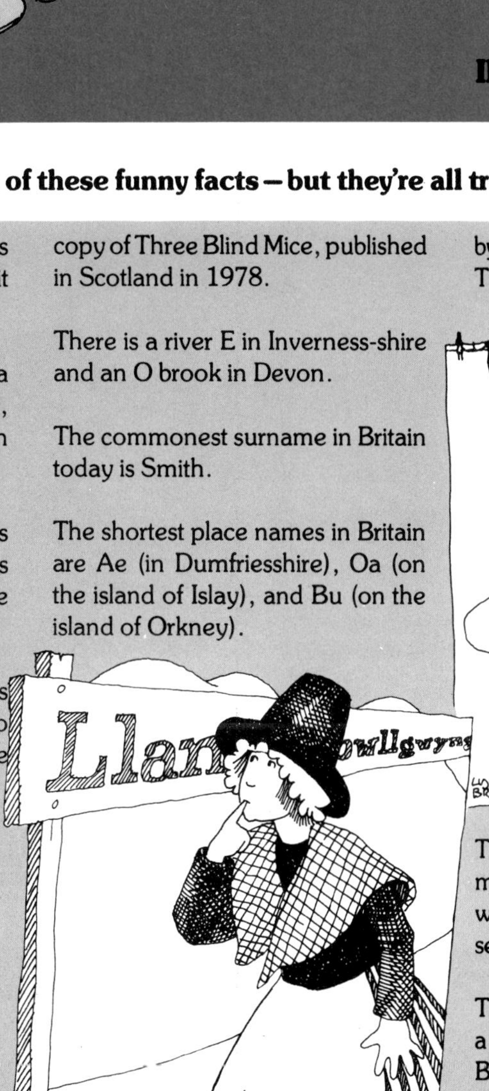

The longest place name in Britain is the Welsh town of—wait for it—Llanfairpwllgwyngyllgogerychwyrndrobwllllantysiliogogogoch! It means 'St. Mary's church in a dell of white hazel trees, near the rapid whirlpool, by the red cave of the Church of Saint Tysilio.' So now you know!

The world's longest daisy chain measured around 1,350 metres and was made in Wales in 1978. It took seven hours to make!

The longest known name belongs to a German man. He is named Adolph Blaine Charles David Earl Frederick Gerald Hubert Irvin John Kenneth Lloyd Martin Nero Oliver Paul Quincy Randolph Sherman Thomas Uncas Victor William Xerxes Yancy Zeus Wolfeschlegelsteinhausenbergerdorff, Senior, but he just calls himself Mr. Wolfe Senior!

A Mr Izumi of Japan has been proved to be 115 years old!

GIRL GUIDES

BE A STAMP COLLECTOR!

The 1977 Wildlife issue.

Start a hobby... be a Collector! You can collect all sorts of things: stamps, postmarks, picture postcards, dolls in national costume, to name just a few!

The nicest thing about working for your Collector's Badge is that having taken your test you not only have another badge, you will have a hobby which may interest you for the rest of your life!

START WITH STAMPS

Philately—better known as stamp collecting—can be quite an inexpensive hobby because you can actually start off your collection with the stamps from the letters which pop through your own door; almost everyone has a letter sometime during the year. You can also ask your relatives for stamps, and penfriends and relatives living abroad are a good source of free foreign stamps. Relatives working in commercial offices, and old letters hidden away in grandma's attic, can produce some unusual stamps, some of which just may be quite valuable too!

Once you have a supply of stamps, you will want to display them to their best advantage. By far the best type of album is a loose leaf album... you can always drop a hint just before your birthday or at Christmas! A loose leaf album usually contains sixty to a hundred cartridge pages, faint quadrille-ruled, to enable the stamps to be mounted neatly. The leaves are held in a spring-back or peg system which allows the removal of sheets in a matter of seconds.

To preserve stamps in good condition, they must be mounted with stamp hinges. These are made from transparent paper, and ready gummed with a pure, tasteless gum, so that they easily peel off from the stamp and album leaf. Other main essentials for your hobby include a magnifying glass—hence the badge symbol—and a pair of tweezers for handling the stamps easily.

ARRANGING YOUR COLLECTION

Arranging your stamp collection is a matter of taste, but certain rules should be followed to achieve an interesting page. Allow no more than five rows of stamps to a page with not more than six stamps in a row. Arranging in patterns is effective, and often it is interesting to give pages over to certain stamp themes such as Christmas, sports, transport, famous people—and so on.

You can get lots of ideas from inspecting the collections of more experienced stamp collectors and also from visiting stamp exhibitions where famous collections are shown. These ideas can be adapted to suit your own tastes.

Some information about the stamps or about their country of origin helps greatly in making your display of interest not only to you, but to your relatives and friends who may inspect your treasures.

MAGPIE MADNESS

You need not collect stamps unless you like the idea... but do save your stamps to send to your favourite charity. Your Brownie Guider will probably have some addresses if you ask her.

If stamps don't appeal, how about starting a collection of book matches, bus tickets, old buttons, dolls house furniture, or even railway timetables!

Whatever you choose to collect, have fun!

FASCINATING FACTS

Although your collection will be started for fun and your own interest, the day may come when you may find that one of your more unusual stamps could be quite valuable! A few years ago, two Guyanan stamps were sold in London for £75,000. Can you imagine paying all that money for two tiny pieces of paper?

The first 'Penny Black', the very first stamp of all, is a true collector's piece, prized as much for its rarity as its value. It had a black picture of the reigning queen of the time, Queen Victoria, on the front... hence the stamp's name.

Adhesive stamps were first introduced in 1840, and the first stamp cost one old penny.

Before that date, 'Post Boys' travelled the length and breadth of the land on foot or on horseback, delivering letters. These were put inside envelopes which were then sealed with wax. In order to read the letter which was addressed, but which had no stamp on, of course, the person who received the letter had to pay a 'delivery charge' for it before the Post Boy handed it over! Poor people were often unable to pay the delivery charge and so did not get letters from, say, a member of the family, who had perhaps gone to a big city in search of work. But the writing on the envelope was enough to show that the wanderer was still safe and well! It was later decided that the delivery charge should be paid by the sender of the letter, and so adhesive stamps were introduced.

In China in 1913, a stamp was issued almost ten inches by three, while among Columbian stamps in the year 1836, there was a stamp measuring only 0.31in by 0.37in.

The 1979 Christmas issue.

These reproductions are by kind permission of the Post Office.

The 1980 Famous People issue.

Wild Animals in the City

By Ann Pinder

Illustrated by Bob Hersey

Nature conservation is often in the news these days, and great efforts are being made to protect the country places in which wild animals and birds make their homes.

Some animals, though, are learning to live in a new kind of habitat: learning to change their ways of life to fit in with those of man, moving closer to the towns and cities which they once avoided. They are changing their feeding habits, and finding new homes in abandoned buildings, even garden sheds.

This is a very good example of the ways in which nature is constantly changing and adapting itself to new conditions. But it certainly does not mean that we should forget about nature conservation: the countryside is still the natural home of birds and animals, and we should do all we can to conserve our fields and woodlands and hedgerows.

Here are some of the animals which now sometimes make their homes in towns. Have you seen any of them there?

TOAD

Look for toads in hidey-holes under stones, in rotting trees, in old walls or in damp cellars. They like to tuck themselves away in cool, dark places to hibernate for winter.

In spring they make their way overland to spawn, but not just to any pond. They return each year to the same stretch of water, even though this may mean a hazardous journey across busy streets. Some nature lovers organise special 'toad crossing patrols', to see the animals safely from one side of the road to the other!

Once the breeding season is over the toads return to land, emerging each evening from their homes to feed on slugs, snails, worms and various insect pests. Toads are good friends to gardeners!

Some people like to keep toads as pets, but it is not really advisable. However, if you see toads regularly in your garden they could become quite tame. They can live to a great age, and you may see the same toad year after year.

KESTREL

If an animal or bird has a sufficient food supply then it will thrive and rear a healthy family. With the kestrel that means plenty of short-tailed voles and other small mammals, and these it finds in grassy banks, for instance at the side of motorways. The kestrel has become a familiar sight to motorists, hovering with pointed wings quivering and tail spread like a fan.

These birds don't build nests, but lay their eggs on cliff ledges, in tree holes, or in the abandoned nests of other birds. In towns they will raise their young on high buildings, or even in windowboxes on blocks of flats. One pair of London kestrels reared two chicks on the sixteenth floor; another pair chose a smart address: The House of Lords.

Keep a lookout for kestrels on your motorway journeys.

PEPPERED MOTH

In 1948 an unusual Peppered Moth was discovered near Manchester. It was not pale in colour like other Peppered Moths, but black. More and more of these dark moths were found, and the reason was found to be pollution.

The Peppered Moth rests on tree trunks which, in a clean atmosphere are covered in a grey-green form of plant life called lichen. Against this background the pale speckled moth was perfectly camouflaged. When man began to use more coal, though, in houses and factories, the air became full of dust and smoke, and the lichen often disappeared. The Peppered Moth became an easy prey for birds, whose sharp eyes soon spotted the pale moths on the dark tree bark. But the darker ones, being better camouflaged, remained unnoticed.

In recent years the atmosphere in cities has greatly improved, so perhaps one day the lichen—and the pale Peppered Moth—will return.

FOX

In stories, the fox is generally cast as a sly rogue, and he certainly has been crafty in moving into the city suburbs. Not only do parks and gardens supply a plentiful supply of insects, birds and small mammals, but the fox has also found another easy food supply in dustbins full of household scraps.

He searches for food at night, sometimes trotting casually down suburban streets and through gardens. Sometimes town dwellers

hear a fox's bark, or find his long-clawed footprints in muddy soil.

During the day the fox hides in cellars or disused buildings, or he may excavate his burrow, called an earth, beneath a garden shed. Sometimes the cubs will be reared in the garden or on a railway embankment.

Some naturalists believe that town foxes are not generally so healthy as their country cousins, for they are smaller, and their fur often looks bedraggled. Country foxes have thick bushy fur, and a magnificent tail, called a brush.

WOODLOUSE

Woodlice belong to the family of crustaceans, which normally live in water. Lobsters and crabs are crustaceans. The woodlouse lives on land, but prefers damp, cool conditions, beneath stones, bricks and bark, and he emerges mostly in the cool of the night.

A crustacean's coat is rather like a suit of armour: it protects its owner's soft body, but doesn't grow with it. Instead it has to be moulted, or cast off, at regular intervals, and the woodlouse does this in two stages. First, it loses the hard skin on its hindquarters, and then, three days later, the skin on its front half comes away. This is why you sometimes see a woodlouse with one half of its body a lighter colour than the other.

Occasionally a woodlouse with a hunched-up back may be found—a sure sign that in a pouch beneath its body it is carrying young, either as unhatched eggs, or as tiny cream-coloured babies, perfect replicas of their parents, who ride along with mum until they are ready to 'leave home'.

PIGEON

Pigeons have lived alongside man for many centuries, since man discovered the wonderful homing abilities of this bird. Ever since, pigeons have provided a valuable messenger service, especially in times of war. Man has also used this bird for food.

The Romans built special pigeon houses called columbaria in which to house the birds, and from Roman times onwards landowners in Britain had pigeon houses in the grounds of their manor houses. You may find one of these buildings—often a circular, towerlike structure—in your local park, which may once have been part of a private estate.

Sometimes pigeon houses were called culveries: the Old English word for pigeon was culfre. Today's town pigeons are probably the ancestors of those birds.

The Woodpigeon is a relative of the town pigeon, and can often be found in town parks and large gardens. They sometimes become tame enough to eat out of your hand.

GREY SQUIRREL

This member of the rodent family has only lived in Britain since 1876, when it was first introduced into Yorkshire from America. The grey squirrel does a lot of damage, eating the bark off trees, and stealing eggs from nests. In parks it will sometimes become quite tame, and many people have squirrels living in their gardens which will take food from the window ledges.

When you are next in the park look out for the squirrel's nest or drey, an untidy bundle of twigs at the top of a tree. This is where the young squirrels are born, in litters of from three to six babies.

In winter the squirrel sleeps a great deal, though it does wake up on warmer days. Watch out for the clawed footprints in the snow, and tell-tale scrapes in the earth where it has searched for the supplies of acorns and nuts it buried in the autumn months.

HEDGEHOG

The next time you find a hedgehog look closely at its spines (but don't touch them!) You will see that they are about 2cm long and tipped with a light yellowy colour.

When alarmed the hedgehog rolls itself into a tight ball with its spines erect, so that it is completely protected from its enemies. Unfortunately, many hedgehogs adopt this means of defence against one of their biggest enemies, the motor car. And in this case it just does not work! It would be far better of course for the hedgehog to run away, particularly as it can run quite fast, despite its short legs.

During the day the hedgehog sleeps under a hedge or in a bramble patch. It comes out for food, and will eat practically anything, from slugs and snails to fallen fruit and crumbs put out for birds! If you have a hedgehog which visits your garden, put out a saucer of bread and milk for it to eat. It may even return at the same time the next day, in the hopes of finding another saucerful!

Come to Noah's Ark

with John Ryan

A couple of years ago, Hamlyn's the publishers asked me to think about writing and drawing some new books for young children. They suggested that they should be about a group of people, and not one special hero. They wanted a story which readers in all sorts of different countries would understand and enjoy. And they wanted animals in the story.

I thought and thought. Then, suddenly, I had the idea that there was one very old story which I could re-write in my own way: the story of Noah and his Ark.

As soon as I started to think about the Ark the characters began to form quite clearly in my mind. Mr and Mrs Noah were a nice comfortable couple. Mr and Mrs Shem were tall and rather mean looking, because they look after all the ship's stores and the money. Mr and Mrs Ham were short, fat and cheerful. Ham is the ship's carpenter and his wife does the cooking.

Then I thought: "Why not make Japeth, the youngest son, into a small boy? It would be more fun for the children reading my stories. And if Shem and Ham had wives it was only fair for

Jaffet (as I called him) to have a girl friend. So I drew Jannet and put her in the story too.

Last of all I added one character who shouldn't really have been on the Ark at all. He is called Crockle and he is a baby crocodile who belongs to the children. There are already two perfectly good (or bad!) crocodiles on board, but Crockle looks so sad when the rain starts that he gets smuggled onto the Ark by friendly Ham in the very first story, and he has exciting adventures in all the Ark books.

I know, of course, that Crockle doesn't come into the real Bible story about the Ark. But sometimes authors allow themselves to twist the truth a little bit, for fun—and actually, I think Crockle is rather nice.

The Noah's Ark books are published by Hamlyn's Beaver Books, and are available from most bookshops.

GIRL GUIDES

Pick a Pattern

Even if you've never tried toymaking before, you'll find it surprisingly easy when you use one of these Style soft toy patterns.

Each of the toys shown here could be made up in an evening. None of them uses much material and they would all make super Christmas presents!

The toys shown on the right are ideal for babies and young children. Perhaps you have a baby brother or sister who would like one? We have made them up in soft fur fabric, but they would also look good made from velvet, terry towelling or any fleecy material. Ask your mother to have a look in her scrap bag, and remember that it is always advisable to use flameproof materials. The toys are stuffed with kapok and their faces and collars are sewn on, so there are no sharp edges for a baby to get hold of. The pattern number to ask for is Style 2826.

The toys on the left are more suitable for older children—in fact you'll probably want to keep them for yourself! Easily made from pieces of coloured felt and a few extras such as buttons, ribbons, etc., their pattern number is Style 2535. The size of these toys when made up is approximately 20cms from head to foot.

Style patterns are available from dressmaking shops and large department stores.

Good luck with your Brownie Toymaker's Badge!

PACK HOLIDAY PICTURE PUZZLE

Devised by Phyllis Mead
Illustrated by Chris Sheridan

A Brownie who was away on Pack Holiday sent this letter to her friend. Can you work out what she wrote?

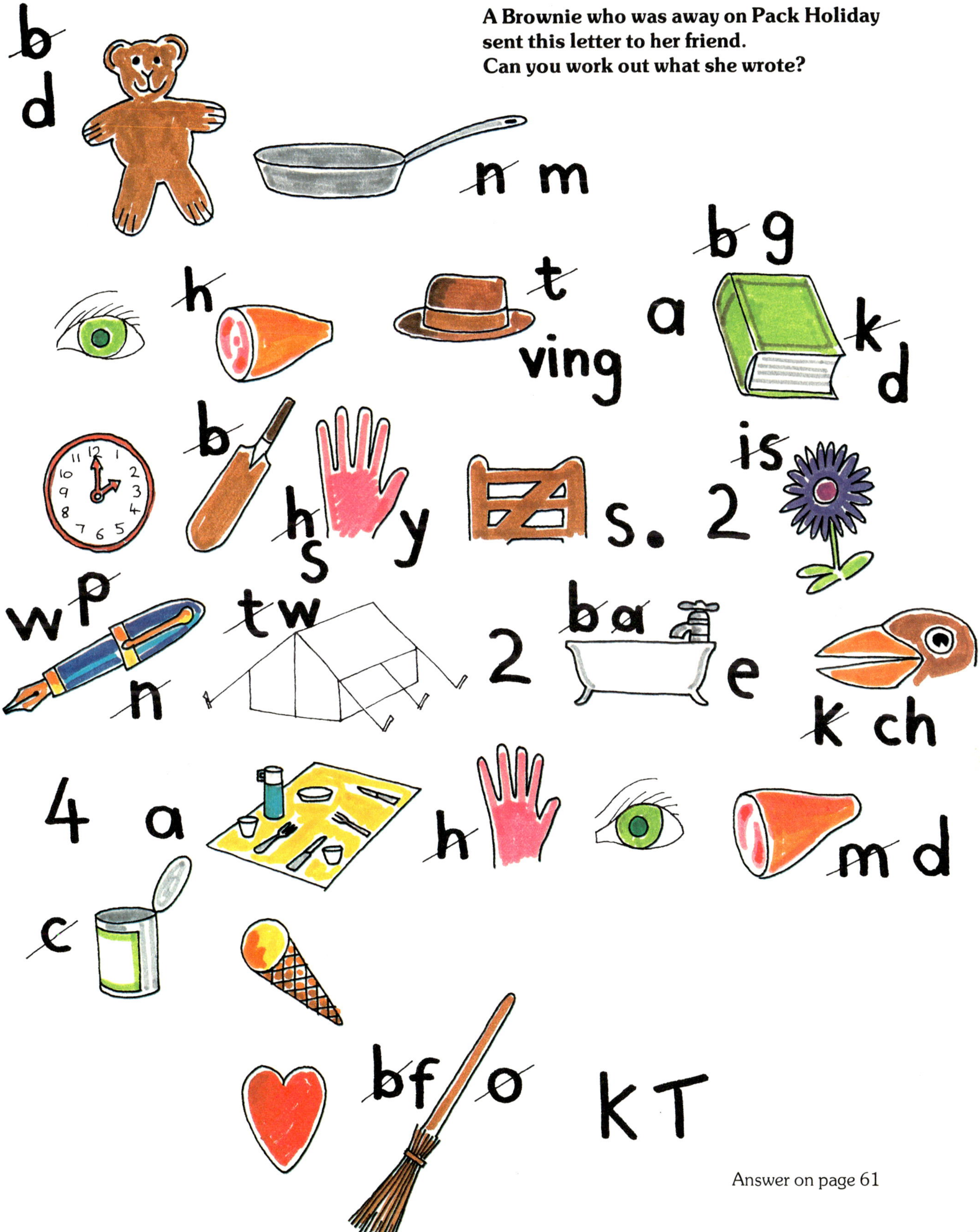

Answer on page 61

Look at Winter

If you look at the pictures of this country scene in the other seasons of the year, you will see two trees which never bore leaf. They were two elms, which had been stricken by the tree disease called Dutch Elm Disease, and now the farmer has had to fell them. The rooks which were nesting up there will have to find another home next spring. Watch out for foxes in winter, when their rich brown coats show up against the snow. Animals need a lot of food in winter, and the sparrowhawk is busily hunting its prey of sparrows and other small birds. The rabbit has just had a lucky escape from a wily weasel, and the pheasants in the field will soon scurry for safety when they see the fox. The song thrush and the redwing are busy too, looking for food. They will eat all earthworms and insects, as well as any nuts, seeds and fruit which they can find. Winter may be the coldest season of the year, but there is still plenty to see in the fascinating world of nature.

ALMOST A GUIDE

By Geraldine Greenhill

"It's from the old we travel to the new", runs a song sung by the Guides. Will you soon be travelling from Brownies to Guides? Maybe you are excited at the thought of joining a friend or an elder sister already in Guides, and you know what fun it's going to be. Or perhaps you are not quite sure about taking this step, and you are wondering what it will be like? Your Brownie Guide Handbook gives some of the things you will be taking with you on your journey up to Guides. One thing you will certainly take with you is your Promise, made as a Brownie. It will continue to grow and you will renew it when you become a Guide and promise to keep the Guide Law.

Let's look at the Guide Laws and at what they mean.

1. A Guide is loyal, and can be trusted.

   This means that you stand up for your family, your friends, your country, your school and your church. Because you are a Guide, people will expect you to be the sort of person they can trust.

2. A Guide is helpful.

   In Guides you will learn more skills, and through them, different ways of being helpful.

3. A Guide is polite and considerate.

   This is another way of saying "think of others before yourself' and put other people's feelings first.

4. A Guide is friendly and a sister to all Guides.

   In Guides you will be widening your circle of friends and learning more about Guides in other countries, and possibly meeting some of them.

5. A Guide is kind to animals and respects all living things.

   It is not kind to overfeed any animal, or to pick wild flowers.

6. A Guide is obedient.

   Not an easy law to keep; how often do we grumble when asked to do a job for mother? But how much nicer if we could do it with a smile!

7. A Guide has courage and is cheerful in all difficulties.

   Here's where that Brownie smile comes in. Some people call it 'putting on a brave face'.

8. A Guide makes good use of her time.

   Try planning out each day to allow time for work and pleasure.

9. A Guide takes care of her own possessions and those of other people.

   This law really needs no explanation, just practising.

10. A Guide is self controlled in all she thinks, says and does.

    Because you think of others first, you learn to control yourself, your thoughts and your actions.

Something to make a noise about – going up to Guides! (North Western Newspapers)

Guides presenting gifts of home-made toys to children in hospital (Thornton Cleveleys Times)

… and having fun dressing up to 'match' this old fire pump (Wiltshire Newspapers)

You will, I am sure, be able to see that all these Laws are basically an extension of your Brownie Guide Law, put in a more grown up way.

I wonder if you have ever Lent a Hand in a Pack Venture to raise money for a special project, like the Guide Friendship Fund or Guide Dogs For The Blind? If so, you have experienced the true meaning of Lending A Hand, or Giving Service, as this part of the Eight Point Programme is known by the Guides. Were you swept along by the great tide of enthusiasm everyone felt? It's a lovely feeling, isn't it—but don't forget the little acts of kindness which are just as important in their own way as the bigger, more organised forms of giving service.

As a Brownie, you will have helped out in various ways, doing what needed doing on the spot, such as fetching the Brownie pool for your Brownie Guider or putting away a piece of equipment. As a Guide, you will continue to look out for jobs that need doing in the Company, but you will also be involved, with your Patrol, in learning how to give service in specialised ways, through a skill such as First Aid or Accident Prevention. You will learn how to BE PREPARED in an emergency. Some Guide Companies have a regular piece of service which they carry out on a monthly basis, like cleaning the church brass, or visiting a housebound person to shop for them or to change their library books. It is important that this type of service is regular—it is no service at all if you forget or can't be bothered to go. Because you are a Guide, people will rely on you to do what you have promised to do.

All this makes giving service appear very grand and important, but don't forget the other side of things—the smaller, needful acts of help given during the course of each day: straightening the rucked mat, picking up pieces of litter, carrying a shopping bag for your mother.

Perhaps your Brownie Guider could arrange for you to visit a Guide Company; if so, do keep your eyes open. Can you discover the signal the Guides use for silence? Brownies are very good at using their imagination, so let's pretend for a moment that we are at a Guide meeting. The Guides are busy in their Patrols—let's join the Kingfisher Patrol and see what they are doing. Their Guider has given them a fire-lighting challenge. They have each collected a handful of matchstick-thin twigs from different trees and are trying to discover how each twig will burn. The beech that Ann has brought is giving a lovely flame, but oh, how Mary's elder twigs smoke! Next week they are planning to light a fire outdoors and to toast marshmallows over the embers.

At Brownies you will have worked for some Challenges during your Brownie Journey on the Footpath, Road and Highway. When you go up to Guides you will find that they also have Challenges. First there is the Pre-Promise Challenge, which you will do to show that you really want to become a Guide, then each year you will work towards an Eight Point badge. With the help of your Patrol Leader (like a Brownie Sixer) and your Guider, you will choose to do new activities from each of the Eight Points, while at the same time trying your best to keep the Guide Promise. All the activities you do at Guides will help you to gain your Eight Point Badge.

I hope you will enjoy taking 'one more step' along the road.

The joys (?) of camping! (Staffordshire Sentinel Newspapers)

Paper Capers!

Have fun making these 'Paper Capers' from Bowater-Scott products.
LEO THE LION AND CEDRIC THE CAT

You will need

- Cores from Fiesta or Scottowels (kitchen towels)
- Yellow Andrex
- An empty Scotties pack—Harmony, Woodland Flowers or Rainbow types
- White Scotties tissues
- Adhesive, such as Pritt
- Yellow paint, black paint and paint brushes
- White crayon and black crayon
- Length of black and length of yellow wool

How to make them

Using the end of the Scottowel or Fiesta core, draw two circles of card from an empty Scotties pack.
Cut out and paint one circle yellow and the other black.
Cut out a rectangular shape, 5cm wide, from an empty Scotties pack and glue it along the length of core from Fiesta or Scottowels, cut to desired length. Repeat once. Paint one shape yellow, the other black.

LEO THE LION

Draw the lion's face on the circle of yellow cardboard and stick it flat onto one open end of the yellow core.

Fold a sheet of yellow Andrex in half lengthwise, and fringe the tissue along the cut edges, making each incision 5cm deep. To make the lion's shaggy mane, stick the fringed tissue around the circular face.

Cut a 10cm length of yellow wool, tie a knot on one end, and stick the unknotted end onto the core to make the lion's tail.

CEDRIC THE CAT

Make the same basic animal shape as above, but glue on two pointed ears cut from the cardboard and painted black. Using a white crayon, draw in the cat's face and make the whiskers out of a white Scotties tissue, fringed, glued on and trimmed.

Cut a 10cm length of black wool and glue on to the other end of the core to make the cat's tail.

ARCHIE THE OCTOPUS

You will need

- One box of Mansize Scotties
- Pipe cleaners
- Adhesive, such as Pritt
- Ribbon
- Rubber bands

How to make him

Head: Make a ball of tissue and cover smoothly with two layers of Mansize Scotties. Secure at the neck with a rubber band.

Legs: Take two pipe cleaners and join them end to end. Place diagonally across the corner of a Mansize Scotties tissue and roll the tissue tightly round. Glue down loose tip of tissue. Do this again twice to make sure pipe cleaner is completely covered. Repeat eight times if your Octopus is to have his full complement of legs!

Flatten the neck of the Octopus, trim off surplus tissue. Secure ends of legs under the neck with glue. Arrange legs, paint face and tie a jaunty ribbon bow round the neck.

WIN A PAINTING SET!

Brownies – Enter our exciting competition!

All you have to do is get out your paints or crayons and draw a picture of your Brownie Pack. They can be at a Pack meeting, or Pack Holiday, or anywhere you like! Draw the picture on a piece of plain paper no larger than 290mm × 210mm. You can use crayons, paints, coloured pencils or felt tips, and the Brownies in your drawing can be in full uniform or in Pack Holiday T-shirts and shorts.

On the back of your drawing clearly print your name, address, age and the name of your Brownie Pack. Also, tell us what you like best about this year's Brownie Annual, and why. Don't forget this part, as it is very important. It helps us to make your annuals better each year.

The first prize is a giant deluxe painting set kindly donated by Reeves Paints. There are also some lovely painting sets for the runners-up. So don't delay—start drawing today!

Send your entries to: The Editor, The Brownie Annual, 17-19 Buckingham Palace Road, London SW1W 0PT.

The closing date for entries is March 31st 1982. The winners will be notified by post, and the Editor's decision is final.

ANSWERS

DOT-TO-DOT BADGES

A—House Orderly; B—Pathfinder; C—First Aid; D—Pony Rider; E—Artist; F—Collector; G—Discoverer; H—Swimmer; I—Cook; J—Signaller

SUITCASE PUZZLE

SIX EMBLEM CROSSWORD

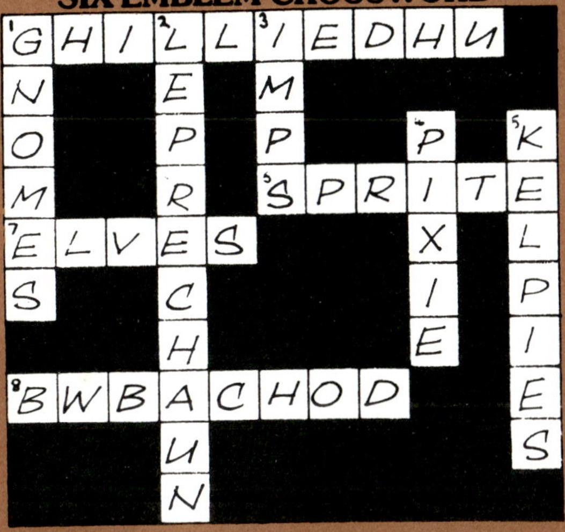

BROWNIE FRIENDS BADGE PUZZLE

1  REPUBLIC OF PANAMA	2  BELGIUM	3  ICELAND
4  REPUBLIC OF CHINA	5  BRAZIL	6  GREECE
7  ISRAEL	8  CANADA	9  SUDAN

PACK HOLIDAY PICTURE PUZZLE

Dear Pam,
I am having a good time at Sandy Gates. Today we went to the beach for a picnic and I had an ice cream.
Love from Katie.

THE BROWNIE

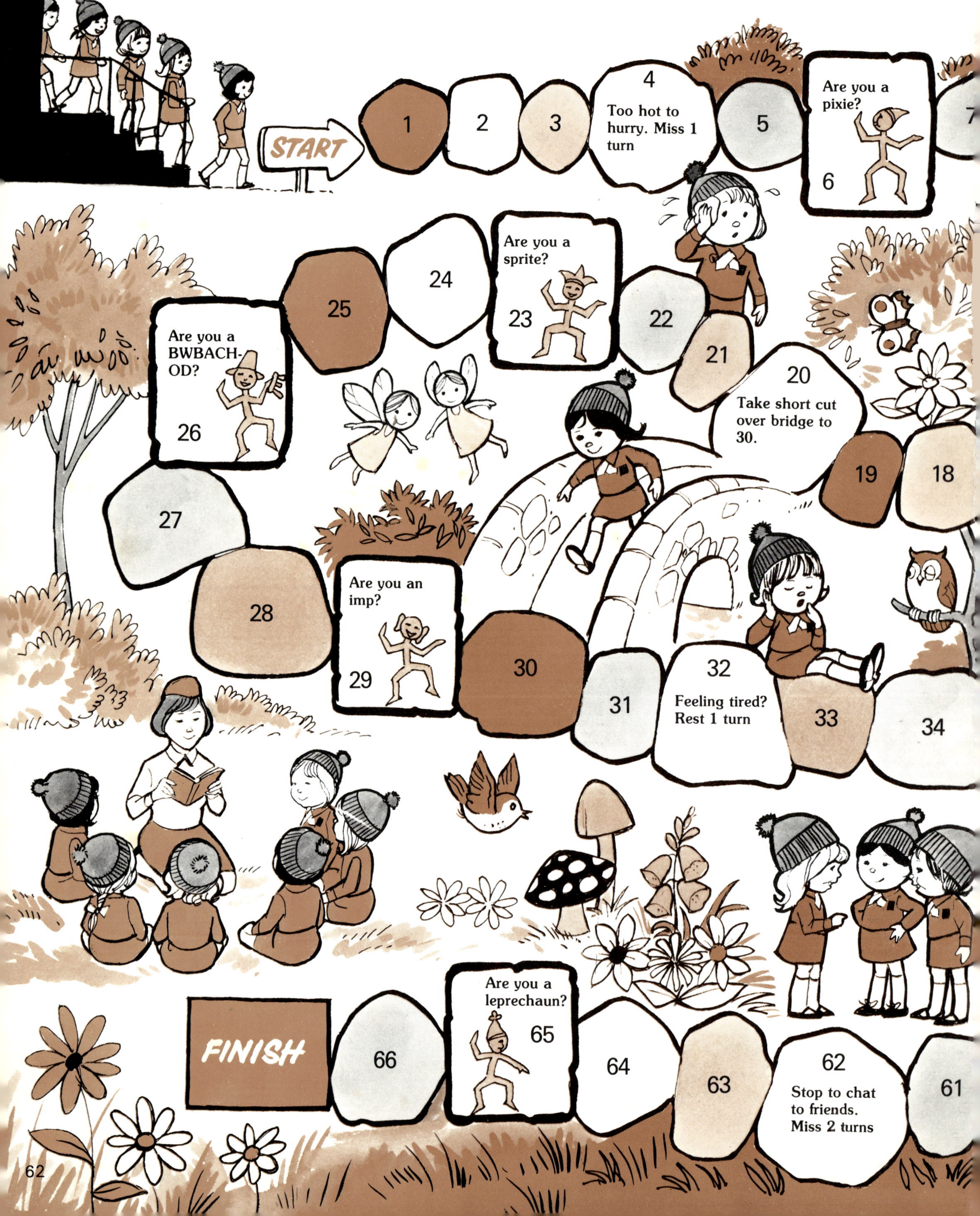

START
1
2
3
4 Too hot to hurry. Miss 1 turn
5
Are you a pixie? 6
7
18
19
20 Take short cut over bridge to 30.
21
22
Are you a sprite? 23
24
25
Are you a BWBACH-OD? 26
27
28
Are you an imp? 29
30
31
32 Feeling tired? Rest 1 turn
33
34
61
62 Stop to chat to friends. Miss 2 turns
63
64
Are you a leprechaun? 65
66
FINISH